The Ethics of Karbala

The Ethics of Karbala investigates the relationship between sacred narratives and the development of character. Focusing on the warrior ethos expressed in accounts of the Battle of Karbala, Zargar searches for the place of the martial virtues in modern life and warfare.

This book is the first of its kind in taking a virtue ethics approach to the study of Islamic history. It offers an ethical analysis of arguably the most pivotal moment in Islamic history. To do so, it makes use of interdisciplinary methods, especially global philosophy and religious studies, and draws on philosophical concepts spanning from Nietzsche to Iqbal. The book's clear and engaging prose makes it accessible to readers seeking a profound understanding of intersections between practical philosophy and religious myths.

This book targets upper-level undergraduate readers seeking to discover Islamic ethics. It will serve nonspecialists, specialists in Shiʿi Islamic studies, and all those interested in Islamic ethics, virtue ethics, cross-cultural philosophy, Nietzsche studies, military science, and religious studies.

Cyrus Ali Zargar is Al-Ghazali Distinguished Professor at the Department of Philosophy, the University of Central Florida, USA. His recent publications include *Religion of Love: Sufism and Self-Transformation in the Poetic Imagination of ʿAṭṭār* and *The Polished Mirror: Storytelling and the Pursuit of Virtue in Islamic Philosophy and Sufism.*

Islam in the World
Series Editors
Katherine Brown, Birmingham University, UK
Jorgen Nielsen, Birmingham University, UK

Freedom of Speech in Universities
Islam, Charities and Counter-terrorism
Alison Scott-Baumann and Simon Perfect

Rivals in the Gulf
Yusuf al-Qaradawi, Abdullah Bin Bayyah, and the Qatar-UAE Contest Over the Arab Spring and the Gulf Crisis
David H. Warren

Al-Ghazālī and the Idea of Moral Beauty
Sophia Vasalou

The Sharia Inquiry, Religious Practice and Muslim Family Law in Britain
Edited by Samia Bano

Contemporary British Muslim Arts and Cultural Production
Identity, Belonging and Social Change
Edited by Sadek Hamid and Stephen H. Jones

The Ethics of Karbala
Myths, Modernity, and Virtues of Nobility
Cyrus Ali Zargar

For more information and a full list of titles in the series, please visit: https://www.routledge.com/Islam-in-the-World/book-series/ITWF

"From the last two decades of the seventh century to today, countless Muslims have mourned the murder of al-Husayn (the noble grandson of the Prophet Muhammad). Their work of mourning, however, refuses the intrigue of political pessimism and cynical reason. Rather, they reflect on their responsibility to uphold justice by coming together to remember and feel something of the Karbala tragedy. Does the living memory of this tragedy have ethical relevance today? Scholar of Islamic philosophy and religious ethics Cyrus Ali Zargar answers a resounding 'yes.' He argues that myths about heroic conduct can help us to grapple with the ethical apathy that has beset contemporary regimes—both our current natures of states and states of nature. Thus, to remember al-Husayn in these troubling times is to renew our collective commitment to courage and sincerity, care, and sacrifice. A must-read for anyone interested in moral exemplars, virtue ethics, and the resources of mourning and melancholia."

Ali Altaf Mian, *Izzat Hasan Sheikh Fellow in Islamic Studies, University of Florida, USA*

"Zargar's pen draws ink from a well that is not of this world. His elegant prose rivals the best of the lyric tradition that grew around the remembrance of Karbala, and the masterful translations interspersed throughout transport the reader to the ritual contexts of these stories. While the book foregrounds the ethical dimension of the Karbala narrative, Zargar has not left its historical, affective, or even mystical dimensions unexamined. In Zargar's hands, the warrior ethos at the heart of the myth of Karbala becomes a poignant critique of modern warfare, late-stage capitalism, and the postmodern human condition. Simply put, the book is peerless."

Aun Hasan Ali, *Assistant Professor of Islamic Studies, University of Colorado Boulder, USA*

"Cyrus Ali Zargar's *The Ethics of Karbala* is a brilliant study of one of the defining moments in all of Islamic history, namely the tragic murder of the grandson of the Prophet in Karbala. A work of astonishing erudition, *The Ethics of Karbala* weaves together elements as disparate as Islamic mytho-poetics, Shi'a spirituality, Islamic ethics, Nietzsche, Marvel heroes, and contemporary war ethics into a coherent narrative. It is sure to become a pioneering model for studying nonmodern ethics in light of modern issues."

Muhammad U. Faruque, *Associate Professor of Global Philosophy, University of Cincinnati, USA*

"*The Ethics of Karbala* is a brilliant gem of a book. It is elegant and exceptionally well-written. Cyrus Zargar's examination of nobility, virtue, and the warrior ethic in Shi'ism constitutes an engaging study of positive forms of masculinity, a sorely needed topic within the academic study of Shi'ism specifically but also within the study of Islam more generally."

Edith Szanto, *Assistant Professor of Religious Studies, University of Alabama, USA*

The Ethics of Karbala

Myths, Modernity, and Virtues of Nobility

Cyrus Ali Zargar

Routledge
Taylor & Francis Group
LONDON AND NEW YORK

First published 2025
by Routledge
4 Park Square, Milton Park, Abingdon, Oxon OX14 4RN

and by Routledge
605 Third Avenue, New York, NY 10158

Routledge is an imprint of the Taylor & Francis Group, an informa business

British Library Cataloguing-in-Publication Data
A catalogue record for this book is available from the British Library

ISBN: 978-1-032-19800-2 (hbk)
ISBN: 978-1-032-20784-1 (pbk)
ISBN: 978-1-003-26519-1 (ebk)

DOI: 10.4324/9781003265191

Typeset in Times New Roman
by codeMantra

Contents

Acknowledgments *ix*

Introduction 1

1 To Know the Warrior: Karbala in the Frame of Virtue Ethics 11

2 Noblest among Us: The Comprehensive Virtue of *Karam* 26

3 A Story of War: Revering the Ahistorical Historical Warrior 41

4 No Sword in Hand: Virtual Soldiers and the Caretakers of Memory 67

Conclusion 83

Bibliography 89

Index 97

Acknowledgments

This book was made possible by institutional support from the Al-Ghazali Endowment in Islamic Studies at the University of Central Florida. In writing it, I benefited greatly from the feedback and support of many. Those include Hamid Algar, Aun Hasan Ali, Muhammad U. Faruque, Christy Flanagan-Feddon, Gregory Lipton, Louis Medoff, Ali Altaf Mian, Saʿdiyya Shaikh, and Abdulkader Tayob. It also includes my family, namely, my wife, my mother, my brothers, my sister, and my two children. Yet to one person above all else do I owe a debt of gratitude. My recently departed mother-in-law Farzaneh Khanom's encouragement and constant concern inspired me at every step. Her character—more than anyone else I know—reflected the ideals I describe in this book. To her this book is dedicated.

Introduction

You walk into a dark room. A group of men, all wearing black, sit weeping. Someone is recounting the story of a battle. Nearby, separated by a curtain, a group of women weep too. Whenever the narrative reaches a crescendo, a noble man meets his death, or an innocent woman or child sees harm, the cries of lament grow louder. What I have described happens every year in gatherings around the world. These gatherings commemorate the trials that happened on one day and concern, above all else, one very important person: al-Ḥusayn, the grandson of the Prophet Muhammad, murdered with a loyal group of followers about 50 years after his grandfather left the world.

There are many questions one might ask about such a gathering. Why has this tradition lasted for almost 1,400 years? From where does it draw its intensity? But my question—the one driving this book—is a very specific one: How does the community benefit ethically from remembering the murder of a noble warrior? That is, as a religious practice such storytelling obviously does more than unite the community. They learn from it. Throughout the story, certain traits take center stage as emphasized for emulation. Nobility, fear of God, heroism, and loyalty serve as examples for all those who listen. Beyond that, though, they have clear and very deep emotional commitments to it. Those who grew up hearing the story need to hear little of it before tears come to their eyes, and they take measures to ensure that their children will be the same.

Before proceeding any further, let me share the story in its simplest form—a brief account of the Battle of Karbala, from which this book derives its focus and its name. The killing of al-Ḥusayn ibn ʿAlī occurred on the tenth day of the month of Muḥarram in the year 61 of the Islamic calendar, or, 13 October, 680 CE. It began with al-Ḥusayn's resistance to the rise of a ruler almost always described as tyrannical and reprobate: the caliph Yazīd I (r. 680–683). At the time, al-Ḥusayn was the Prophet Muhammad's only living grandson, so his allegiance mattered to the legitimacy of the young ruler. When al-Ḥusayn refused to pay such allegiance, the caliph's forces pursued him. Matters intensified after al-Ḥusayn, his family, and a small group of supporters were cornered in Karbala, Iraq, upon the orders of a local governor appointed by

DOI: 10.4324/9781003265191-1

Yazīd. At that location, most of the men, including al-Ḥusayn, were killed in an uneven battle forced upon them. Accounts of the battle describe men on that day embracing their death at the hands of the soldiers who outnumbered them, because of their absolute loyalty to al-Ḥusayn and love for him and his family. The governor's forces murdered al-Ḥusayn and his sons, one of whom was an infant, with particular cruelty. With al-Ḥusayn killed, these forces took the remaining women and children captive, along with an adult son of his who was too infirm to fight. Shiʿi sacred narratives usually remember the event as an act of idealistic self-sacrifice, and Sunni narratives have largely—with some exception—agreed.[1] Moreover, both Shiʿi and Sunni Muslims have commemorated al-Ḥusayn's martyrdom, through poetry, dramatic reenactments, sermons, and other forms of communal grief that intensify on the tenth of the month of Muḥarram, known as the Day of ʿĀshūrā.[2]

The Storied Past of a Warrior Ethos

As to why all this matters, understanding the remembrance of this battle might help us uncover something about our moral situation today, a situation of ever-present wars, but an often-absent warrior, at least "warrior" in the traditional sense. I do not intend to imply that the event of Karbala is sui generis, that is, somehow so different from other narratives that it offers something completely unique. Nor do I intend to advocate that my audience learn from the narrative of Karbala, its remembrance, or the community who partakes in that remembrance. Not directly. Rather, I want to think of it as an incredibly powerful case study for a type of narrative—that of the metaphysically favored warrior-hero—that predominated much of premodern life. The *lack* of such heroic narratives interests me most: What happens when we have no such stories to remember?

The celebrated ethicist MacIntyre deals with a similar problem in his book, *After Virtue.* He describes heroic societies (in his case, the ancient Greeks) as valuing certain traits, such as courage, and not valuing others, such as humility. Some of those traits might surprise us.[3] I remember, as a five-year-old in the midwestern United States, being told by my teacher that "men do not cry," having split my chin open on the pavement during recess. In many heroic societies, however, men do cry. In the story of al-Ḥusayn, men weep profusely. They weep at the loss of friends and family, or at the injustice wrought upon al-Ḥusayn. In ancient Greek heroism, that of Homer's *Iliad,* men wept over the loss of friends too—as did horses. Their masculinity was not at risk for such weeping.[4] Part of what interests me in these narratives is in their ability to foster masculinities and femininities that thrive in settings of selflessness, and yet also experience deeply expressed emotions of care.

In a sense, this book will contrast two types of culture, but these types of culture are two imperfect things, almost impossible to define. The cold reality is that neither of these existed or exists in any neat way. They are imagined—but usefully imagined, because they help us make sense of the cultural trends we see now and read about in the past or among others. On the one hand are the heroic narratives and heroic cultures that gave us stories like that of Karbala. On the other hand are nonheroic cultures. The philosopher Friedrich Wilhelm Nietzsche (d. 1900) took interest in nineteenth-century Europe as a place of such nonheroic cultures, yet one that had had a heroic past. A major factor in the decline of heroic values among Europeans, according to Nietzsche, was Christianity. So much so, that Nietzsche took great interest in Islam, hoping to find in that religion a living version of the cultural strengths that Europe had lost and was continuing to lose. How right Nietzsche was in his assessment of Islam can be debated, or, more precisely, in many ways he was quite wrong. Yet his efforts give us a way to begin this exploration of heroism, the warrior, and religious narratives.

The "heroism" under investigation (which I will call a "warrior ethos" and, specifically in its Islamic context, "warrior nobility") resides exclusively in no particular culture. It also lacks in no particular culture, at least as far as I know. Moreover, within an overarching culture, a subculture might show awareness of the lack of such heroism and search for it within another subculture. After all, a society, nation, or people can contain within it multiple cultures. An acknowledgment of one or some of those subcultures as more heroic than others is really a culture commenting on itself. Or this might occur when two cultures encounter each other. After the Mongol invasions ravaged Western Asia, for example, satirist ʿUbayd Zākānī (d. ca. 1370) responded to the failed courage of Muslim men in his satirical treatise *Virtues of the Noble* (*Akhlāq-i ashrāf*). He described courage as an "abrogated practice," replaced by a new ethos in which men flee from any risk of killing or being killed, choosing instead weddings, feasts, and dances. In his treatise, traits of warriors became associated with the Mongols, while traits of cowards apply to his own vanquished community of Persian-speaking Muslim men. Both were living together, but, for the satirist, the dominance of one over the other stemmed from the inherent superiority of collective courage over collective cowardice.

As an example from contemporary American popular culture, take the case of Los Angeles as depicted in the 2016 comedy *Keanu*. In the film, a man searches for his stolen kitten. Accompanied by his best friend, he delves into the underworld of armed drugged dealers, only to discover that a very dangerous man has also become attached to the cat. To win back his beloved pet, he and his friend assume the guise of these gangsters. They begin to speak and act in stereotypically tough ways, as they are asked to lead a crew of criminals. Previously, in their normal lives, both had suburban and even quite effeminate demeanors. Having assumed their new roles, however, they discover a source of strength. The protagonist can overcome bullet wounds, fight fearlessly, and even successfully court a female gangster. His friend acquires the ability to stand up in defense of his own wife, who now finds him irresistible.

The film establishes several contrasts: the suburbs versus the inner city, whiteness versus blackness, professionalism versus outlawry, weakness versus strength, unmanliness versus manliness, and cowardice versus bravery. These traits exist in two different geographical and social locations, that is, in two different worlds. Our protagonists traverse from one world into the other, but the film implies that—for most—life exists in either one world or the other. Much of the film is a commentary on America's distinctive social situation today, its cities and suburbs, and perceptions of its criminal underworld. But, on a larger scale, the film's division of traits between admirable outlaws and wimpy citizens reflects a more common human phenomenon found in much of the urbanized world: When armed power becomes the prerogative of the state, unsanctioned warriors can only exist as outlaws and gangsters.

Traditional warrior systems of life have often, historically, given way to centralized authority, that is, the state. Such was the case in Western Europe when the feudal warrior cultures—famous for their knights—became replaced by centralized authority.[5] The loss of this way of life mattered enough to Europeans that it propelled Miguel de Cervantes's (d. 1616) novel, *Don Quixote*, to literary fame. Western Asia, too, has not been immune to the centralization of power and shifts in the social positioning of warriors—again, one related to urbanization. In this region and in the Islamic era, the earliest recorded period of heroic gangs is about 150 years after the Prophet Muhammad's lifetime. Well before they arose, during the years of Muhammad's own lifetime and the decades that followed, matters had been different. Many of the Prophet's own companions bore arms, just as he did, and participation in battle was a general affair for many. Yet by this time, 150 years later, things had changed. We might describe the emergence of a "state," wherein soldiers were professionals or enslaved. Most of these civilians, who were citizens of expanding cities, had no involvement whatsoever in ongoing battles.

In these new circumstances, in a manner like contemporary gangs, these bands of young men had initiation rituals, as well as rituals that consolidated group cohesion. One of these acts was drinking salt water, which might have been borrowed by Muslim gangsters from pre-Islamic Persian knights, who had a very similar ritual involving wine.[6] They lived by a subversive code, which was, in its own way, quite heroic: Protect women, act bravely always, be honest, but also drink wine, go on hunts, enjoy feasts, and recite erotic poetry.[7]

It was with this subversive potential in mind that the governor of Iraq, Khālid ibn ʿAbdallāh al-Qaṣrī (r. ca. 723–738), made a decree forbidding their gatherings.[8] A band of these "scoundrels" (*shuṭṭār*) or "bandits" (*ʿayyārān*) even murdered the great philosopher Abū Naṣr al-Fārābī in 950, during one of their highway robberies.[9] In some renditions, they were called "young men" (*aḥdāth* or *fityān*), and their strength in numbers, commitment to group solidarity, and zeal eventually rendered them a political force as well.

In Syria, aristocrats would vie for their support, and a group of "bandits" even took control of the major Islamic capital of Baghdad in 972.[10]

Eventually, however, these young men were brought into the fold. None other than the caliph joined their ranks, even naming himself to be the head of their organization. This happened in 1207, and the Abbasid caliph in question, al-Nāṣir (r. 1180–1225), seemed to know what to do: He recruited widely respected holy men, especially leaders of Sufi circles, to participate in bringing these fraternal organizations into the domain of the law and hence the state.[11] This process led to the institutionalization of what was once gangsterism, so that these *futuwwa* ("youngmanliness") orders became popular equivalents to Sufi orders. That is, while expectations for pious rigor were rather high in Sufi orders, a man could join a *futuwwa* or *akhī* order and enjoy certain social and devotional privileges, while still maintaining a laxer approach to the spiritual way.[12]

Notice the pattern here. There is an early time of accepted heroism. A wide array of able-bodied men remains ready to participate in battle. Then matters for that society become bigger and more complicated: Men and women work and live protected by professional soldiers, or the police; the city becomes a fortress; and displays of battle-readiness are controlled, limited to the professionals. In response, heroism—or some perceived version of it—becomes reimagined by those who have no legal right to it. They become gangsters or bandits. It then becomes the prerogative of the powers that be to try to control this new expression of armed strength. It does so through metaphors: Bravery means standing up to one's lower passions; strength means overcoming the ego; and the battles that are waged now are against temptation or oneself, not an external enemy. The warrior ethos becomes allegorized.

This very social trend has left its mark on English-language terms to describe character and morality. The English word "virtue" derives from the Latin word *vir*, meaning "man." From this was derived *virtus*, meaning "manliness" or "martial courage."[13] When the word carried this battle-ready meaning, women or the enslaved could not generally possess *virtus*, aside from exceptional cases where they acted like free men. Women, instead, were expected to strive for a type of modesty called *pudicitia*.[14] Yet as Roman society changed, as it shifted from a collection of warriors to a collection of citizens protected by warriors, *virtus* began to mean a more general sense of moral excellence. We put this sense of *virtus* to use when we use its derivative, "virtue," in English. The Roman *virtus* was like the Greek word *arete*, which underwent a similar semantic shift, from a virtue of warriors to virtue in a more general sense. The process of Christianization—during the late Roman Republic—also left its mark on *virtus*, so that self-control, a sort of moral restraint, became the defining trait of noble individuals.[15] Nietzsche was very sensitive to this process. In fact, his resistance to it and interest in correcting it formed a major part of his philosophical outlook. In Chapter 3, I will consider his attempt at cultural remediation for a Europe lacking in the warrior ethos.

Recognizing an Exemplar

Karbala and its cultural remembrance bring to life the warrior ethos in a morally balanced and metaphysically empowered way. This is not, of course, a statement of fact. It is this author's opinion, though an informed opinion belonging to someone who has spent the better part of his adult life studying religion, literature, and—often—religious literature, as well as this particular narrative. In the coming pages, then, I will offer my reasoning for this statement. That is, I will offer a justification for focusing on Karbala as an exemplar myth for a warrior ethos and act of remembrance that can serve as a form of cultural therapy for many of us whose cultures have little place for traditional warrior virtues. Much of that suitability comes from Karbala's situation as a narrative that *avoids* the pitfalls of warrior traits, such as the promotion of violence, the justification of patriarchal attitudes, the failure of merciful attributes, and the discouragement of intellectual inquiry. Narratives resembling the Karbala narrative allow those who remember them to keep the warrior ethos from receding into underground expressions—often dangerous ones, often valued by young men. Instead, they offer a gender-balanced, ethically sound, and philosophically informed version of the warrior ethos.

Throughout, the narrative bears with it a code of nobility, one that must always be present for the warrior and one that has been sanctioned by the divine commands revealed to Muhammad. In one example, a general named al-Ḥurr ibn Yazīd stood on the wrong side of the fight. He stood against al-Ḥusayn. This general, al-Ḥurr, stopped al-Husayn and his retinue on their way to Kufa. When al-Ḥusayn and his retinue requested that al-Ḥurr allow them to settle at a place with water, a town from which they might take rations, al-Ḥurr refused. "No, by God," al-Ḥurr told them, "I cannot, for this man over here has been appointed to spy on me."[16] The narrative here highlights the duress under which al-Ḥurr operates. He is a good soldier, taking commands from an unworthy governor.

Faced with no option of escape, one of al-Ḥusayn's soldiers—Zuhayr ibn al-Qayn—made a practical suggestion to al-Ḥusayn. If al-Ḥurr would not let them settle in a reasonable place, then why not fight them here and now, before the rest of the enemy forces arrive? "O son of God's messenger," Zuhayr said, "Fighting these men here will be much easier than fighting whoever comes after them, for, by my life, an army is coming after these you see over whom we will have no power [to resist]."

Al-Ḥusayn's response to his soldier encapsulates the warrior ethos: "I will not be the one to start fighting." We might naturally have the tendency to read a statement such as this as a declaration of a certain Islamic just war theory. Since just wars must be defensive, initiating the attack would be sinful. Certainly, such a reading cannot be ruled out. It is, however, the phrasing of al-Ḥusayn's response—one that highlights his own character ("*I* will not be the one…") that leads us to see this as a standard that applies to al-Ḥusayn as the noble son of God's messenger, the consummate warrior-leader. Other details within the narrative help us to see al-Ḥusayn's actions as motivated by a disposition, and not by a superimposed set of rules. There are, for example, the relatively peaceful relations that al-Ḥusayn maintains with his enemy al-Ḥurr. At one point, al-Ḥusayn provides water to al-Ḥurr's camp and invites them to pray with him in unison. Indeed, al-Ḥusayn's noble actions eventually lead to al-Ḥurr's conversion and a complete reversal: The enemy general al-Ḥurr meets his end fighting to defend al-Ḥusayn. The response here to Zuhayr ("I will not be the one to start fighting") implies that to fight al-Ḥurr and his troops, at this stage, is both ignoble and treacherous. It would be unexpected and hence beneath the dignity of the Prophet's grandson, al-Ḥusayn. A very different response would be, "It is wicked to begin the fighting" or "the law prohibits aggression."

Al-Ḥusayn's response might be compared to a verse of the Quran that also conveys this warrior ethos: "Fight, for God's cause, those who fight you, but do not overreach. God does not love the overreachers."[17] The verse in question focuses on the person, not the action. Those who habitually transgress bounds are people with the trait of aggression. They are the "overreachers" (*al-muʿtadīn*), burdened by a vice that does not befit God's people, in that they habitually overreach. The verse centers God's "love" or "favor." This directs the reader's attention toward being the sort of person whom God would love, not on following a set of laws. God loves you; God does not love the overreachers; therefore, you must not be an overreacher. I return to this theme in Chapter 2.

The Karbala narrative also shows us how the warrior virtue can thrive in a context that rejects patriarchy as arbitrary authority, even while embracing patrilineage. In other words, the narrative certainly places heroism and nobility within one family, a family whose culture mostly traces lineage and nobility through a line of fathers. (One significant exception to this is that al-Ḥusayn's inherited nobility comes to him both through his father and through his mother, who was the Prophet Muhammad's daughter.) Nevertheless, while a line of fathers matters, the narrative reveals the wickedness of men who rule only by means of force or coercion, while making patriarchal claims to tribal rule. Conversely, the narrative offers an example of a noble female who fights not with arms but by her intelligence and eloquence. That figure is Zaynab, sister to al-Ḥusayn, who was probably around 54 years old when these events took place—less than one year younger than her brother al-Ḥusayn.

After her brothers, sons, nephews, and supporters were murdered, Zaynab was taken before one of the main instigators of those murders, the governor of Kufa, ʿUbaydallāh ibn Ziyād. Ibn Ziyād did not recognize her. When her identity was brought to his attention, the governor remarked: "Praise be to God who disgraced you, killed you, and negated your fabling chatter."[18] By this Ibn Ziyād meant to highlight that Zaynab's brother's claims to authority—indeed all claims to the special status of the Prophet Muhammad's family—had been nullified by al-Ḥusayn's defeat at Karbala. Ibn Ziyād's statement came from an understanding that God had foreordained that Ibn Ziyād, the caliph Yazīd, and their tribe—the tribe of Banū Umayya (or "Umayyads")—would be in power. In fact, the proof of God's will, for Ibn Ziyād, lay in the fact that he was in power: If God did not will him and his people to be in power (and to defeat al-Ḥusayn), then they would not be in power.

Her response completely subverted the power dynamic, shifting the discussion from worldly power (which Ibn Ziyād had) to divinely sanctioned rank (which she and her family had), by citing Quranic evidence:

> Praise be to God who honored us through Muhammad and *purified* us *thoroughly*. It is not as you say. He only disgraces the transgressor and negates the dissolute one.[19]

For Zaynab, the moral purity that God confirmed in the Quran for the Prophet and his family, a moral purity that extended to his granddaughter Zaynab, rendered them an ethical elite, whether or not they held worldly power. God's disgracing of a person differed from the tragedy that had unfolded for the Prophet's family. When God wished to disgrace a person, that person's evil came to light—not their inability to resist brute force.

Ibn Ziyād then responded, "So how do you see what God has done to your household (*ahl baytik*)?" Zaynab's reply articulated her resignation at God's decree—since a person dies at the time of His choosing—and her firm conviction that things would be set right on the Judgment Day:

> Murder had been decreed (written) for them. So they came out proudly to their places of rest. And God will soon bring you and them together (for judgment), so you will all bring your proofs to Him and argue your cases before Him."[20]

At this, Ibn Ziyād grew angry and began "fuming with rage." He could not respond, however, because—as he was reminded—"she is only a woman."[21] In other words, Zaynab forced Ibn Ziyād to face the conundrum of empty patriarchal power. If he continued to engage with her, then he would have acknowledged that her arguments merited a rebuttal. The argument itself would have put the governor on equal footing with a woman, making them equal contenders for truth, or adversaries in debate. Yet he needed to convey that his authority needed no justification and that her words were meaningless outbursts. In this, he represents the coercion model of male authority very often associated with political and military rule. Zaynab, on the other hand, conveys the moral nobility inextricable from Karbala's warrior ethos.

This warrior narrative has a structure that combines service to a transcendent being, self-sacrifice, patience, and nobility, while also negating coercion, mercilessness, arbitrary domination, and entitlement. Yet one other important factor remains. This narrative is alive, part of an ongoing tradition that spans the globe. Particularly for Shiʿi Muslims, this narrative survives as an essential component in pious and ritual life, wherever those Muslims might be found. Iran has the largest population of Shiʿi Muslims, but Iraq, Lebanon, Pakistan, Saudi Arabia, Bahrain, and many other Muslim-majority countries are home to those who commemorate the Karbala narrative yearly and sometimes more frequently than that. Moreover, countries without a Muslim majority, too, have natives and immigrants who put into practice the sort of rituals that I described at the very beginning of this introduction.

The final part of this book will make a case for the warrior ethos in contemporary life. War is one manifest situation in which the waning of the warrior ethos and its myths matters. That the warrior ethos might be in peril has been a key concern of those who study war, conflict, and ethics. The use of drones means that warfare will increasingly involve less physical risk, limited human interaction, and fewer opportunities for merciful conduct. The mechanization of warfare, then, diminishes the human ethical element from war, which, aside from the warrior ethos, has often been among our darkest moments as a species.

The Karbala narrative and the warrior ethos also help us think about the systems by which decisions of war are made and executed, the shape of our political order. The warrior ethos assumes moral elites, as we will see. Yet the modern democratic state often involves the replacement of a moral elite, who were once experts in virtue, by technocrats and a sense of egalitarianism, an argument that I extend from the work of Jeff Mitchell.[22] This results in the waning of culturally specific virtues. Ultimately, the dearth of viable warrior ethos myths, and their unsuitability to many contemporary contexts, presents a crisis in virtue, and contemporary substitutes are mostly placeholders—not real replacements. Video games and films, for example, certainly offer heroism. Yet their themes of fantasy and nationalism lack the metaphysical substance of traditional warrior ethos myths. This affects all those who might find models of emulation in the warrior, whether soldiers or civilians. The warrior ethos can possibly provide a refuge from the moral deterioration of modern life.

This book is an explorative essay in the sense that it only begins to elaborate an idea. It asks a "what if" question about the way a set of compound virtues—the warrior ethos—functions in a sacred narrative, with implications for the way analogically similar narratives have traditionally functioned in human societies. I do often offer evidence, but every argument made herein mostly expands on an idea, namely, that warrior myths resembling the Karbala narrative perform a function needed but often lacking in societies that consider themselves modern. The objective, then, is to explore and wonder, so that perhaps in future studies the question raised here can be scrutinized, analyzed, developed, and perhaps even ultimately answered.

Notes

1 Shoshan (2004, 235).
2 Reid (2011).
3 Sophia Vasalou (2019) studies the difficult reception of the Greek virtue of "greatness of soul" (*megalopsychos*) among Muslim philosophers whose tradition emphasized humility.
4 Föllinger (2009, 24).
5 Elias (2000, 191–194).
6 Zakeri (1995, 310–311).
7 Ridgeon (2010, 21–22); Maḥjūb (1999, 565–568).
8 Maḥjūb (1999, 564–565).
9 Maḥjūb (1999, 568–569); Salinger (1950, 490).
10 Cahen (1958, 245–246); Vryonis (1965, 47); Maḥjūb (1999, 570–571).
11 Ohlander (2008, 26, 272, 286–291).
12 Ohlander (2008, 289–290).
13 McDonnell (2006, 10, 71).
14 Barton (2001, 41); McDonnell (2006, 159–165).
15 McDonnell (2006, 293, 330).
16 al-Ṭabarī (2008, 5:276). All translations in this book are mine unless otherwise indicated.
17 Quran 2:190.
18 al-Ṭabarī (2008, 5:308–309).
19 al-Ṭabarī (2008, 5:309). The italicized words reference Quran 33:33.
20 al-Ṭabarī (2008, 5:309).
21 al-Ṭabarī (2008, 5:309).
22 Mitchell (2019).

1 To Know the Warrior

Karbala in the Frame of Virtue Ethics

This chapter begins an attempt to read Karbala through the lens of a branch of practical philosophy called "virtue ethics." Of course, speakers and writers around the world have been reading this narrative ethically for centuries: Karbala's moral lessons constitute a core concern of sermons, lectures, poems, and books commemorating al-Ḥusayn and his supporters, especially in Shiʿi Muslim circles.[1] Often the focus is on the desirable character traits, or virtues, of al-Ḥusayn and his supporters, as well as the reprehensible traits, or vices, of his foes. Here, however, my audience need not be Shiʿi, nor Muslim, nor even religiously committed. Rather, the goal is to consider Karbala in a virtue ethics framework that would interest all those who study ethics, as it has become defined in universities, journals, and academic associations around the world.

Karbala as Historical Myth

Karbala's ability to effect change within human character—its ethical drive—has always resulted from the beauty of its narrative, as well as the many micronarratives, or personal accounts, within the larger story. That story can be called a "historical myth." On the one hand, the events at Karbala have historical veracity, since they happened in the general way described. We know this because the Karbala narrative comprises a widely reported series of events in the earliest period of Islamic history.[2] Indeed, the first historiographical accounts of Karbala correspond to an "assassination narrative" genre of literature (*maqtal*) that would become the model for later Arabic historical writing.[3] In this sense, Karbala is "historical," or, in other words, confirmed by multiple credible reports. On the other hand, it is also "myth," because of the devotional, ethical, and metaphysical dimensions read into the narrative. Myths bring together devotional communities. Those communities hold this narrative as sacred, that is, as set apart from other narratives or "special" in some way. As such, through poetry, storytelling, and other living ethical practices, those communities have brought dimensions of interpretation to this historical event.[4] Indeed, as myth, the Karbala narrative remembered in sermons and poems can often include insights that have come by way of

DOI: 10.4324/9781003265191-2

dreams or otherworldly inspiration. With an eye on such mythic dimensions, my interests remain in the event's remembered legacy or what might be called its "mnemohistory."[5]

One important note about this narrative is that, as history, it certainly lends itself to a careful and critical approach to sources. Most reports that comprise the Karbala narrative, as well as most of the quotations I cite below, rely heavily on accounts reported by Abū Mikhnaf Lūṭ ibn Yaḥyā (d. 774), whose version comes to us as preserved by the Abbasid historian Muḥammad ibn Jarīr al-Ṭabarī (d. 923) and by many others, as Abū Mikhnaf became recognized as the "principal authority" on the event.[6] My interest in al-Ḥusayn's remembered legacy has meant that I have taken the liberty of including any relevant reports, without interest in evaluations of a historiographical nature.

Because it is considered sacred by those who remember it, a historical myth has a powerful ability to affect those who embrace it, forming their character and even shaping the values and practices of cultures. Historical myths can be ethically transformative. Moreover, the Karbala narrative presents moral agents making life-or-death decisions, sacrificing their lives, and doing so in the name of a transcendent reality and a present human embodiment of prophetic authority. It has much to tell us, in other words, from the perspective of religious ethics.

The Relationship between Ethics and Narrative

To read sacred narratives for models of virtue is common to religious traditions around the world. Moses in Judaism, Jesus in Christianity, and Siddhārtha Gautama in Buddhism might strike the reader as common examples, three among an endless number. Yet, even without a sacred element, narratives have philosophical potential. To reflect on this potential, merely consider the complexity of human motivations, abilities, and decisions. Think about how a concept such as "bravery" might be incredibly complex. Compare the decision to cease life support made by a child with deep religious commitments with that same decision made by a spouse who married an elderly, wealthier person and is now their sole heir. Now think about how a narrative might show us that the child's decision came from a place of spite, while the spouse's decision came from a place of love. That is, imagine the child was subjected to a lifetime of neglect, while the love between the two spouses was rare and real. Now imagine how the spouse's bravery might appear differently in different contexts, such as when having to defy the judgment of others to marry a much older person. Because of such complexities, argues the philosopher Alasdair MacIntyre, humans make sense of moral positions through narratives, for narratives can convey that complexity.[7] It is for these reasons, and others, that the potential of narratives to serve as fodder for thinking about how to "be" has recently captured the attention of moral philosophers.

Narratives and virtue ethics have one important commonality. Both usually stress moral agents over their acts or, rather, stress their lived contexts over any universal laws that might apply to them. In virtue ethics, a situational approach to morality focuses on how one might "be" the best person they can be—as opposed to what they should or should not "do." Narratives describe our circumstances, motivations, and perspectives. They tell us why a person decides a certain way within a certain context and thus what it says about that person's character. They also illustrate how unlikely it is to have one set of norms or rules that applies to everyone, since context varies so widely.

Virtue Ethics: What Is It?

Virtue ethics represents a return to Aristotelian thinking in American and European philosophy. There had been a period after the eighteenth century, when Europeans tried to develop models of morality more rational than what was offered by the ancient Greeks. Largely, they fell into two camps. One camp, a school of thinking that began with Immanuel Kant (d. 1804), argued for a morality of rationally grounded duties. The other camp, the Utilitarian camp, tried to develop a morality based on pleasure, in opposition to the Kantians. Its most important philosophers were Jeremy Bentham (d. 1832) and his student John Stuart Mill (d. 1873). The philosophies of these two camps, especially the latter, shaped much of American and European morality and law up to the present. Yet, around a century ago, Anglo-American or analytic philosophers began to offer a third alternative, having grown weary of the failures of the Kantian and Utilitarian perspectives to fulfill the claims they made for a universal ethics.

G.E.M. Anscombe (d. 2001) had much to do with the third alternative that would arise in the twentieth century, virtue ethics. Her arguments began with her disappointment in Enlightenment arguments made about morality, by Kant, Bentham, Mill, and others, arguments based on a lack of precision about terms and a set of assumptions about responsibility. Anscombe saw the remnants of Christianity and religious obligations in Kant's thought, lingering there in a dishonest sort of way, presenting itself as rationally free from the confines of religion, when, in fact, it was not. From where else (but religion) would Kant derive any sense of "ought"? Instead, returning to psychology, human flourishing, and justice might allow philosophers to do for those alive today what Aristotle had done for ancient Greek nobles, namely, argue for virtues and vices that suit our minds and our social conditions.[8] This would elevate the well-being of the moral agent above any imagined sense of obligation. Philippa Foot, Alasdair MacIntyre, and others have furthered this line of thinking.

Virtue ethicists, then, take more interest in considering how each person can be the best version of themselves they can be, within a context of virtues that we might agree on. Those virtues lead to a good life, that is, they allow a person and a society to flourish. An important concept among virtue ethicists is practical wisdom, or *phronesis*, an interiorized mastery of doing the right thing at the right time. The use of a Greek term should come as no surprise: Much of virtue ethics centers the thought of Aristotle, because of his careful consideration of what constituted the good life in his time and place.

In this book, though, I do not argue for virtue ethics as some alternative to other moral philosophies. Rather, virtue ethics matters here in the sense that any moral philosopher might be interested in virtues and vices—even as complementary to Kantian or Utilitarian ethics, or as complementary to religious ethics, such as Islamic law. Nevertheless, any such discussion would be impossible without the progress that has been made in virtue ethics in the past century, which has provided the foundations for this discussion.

Can We Really Learn from Historical Warrior Narratives in an Ethical Sense?

Before we look closely at the Karbala narratives, I must address one of the most significant problems in virtue ethics, a problem that pertains to studying Karbala through the lens of virtue ethics. Karbala, after all, is an event that occurred nearly 1,400 years ago. The primary philosopher associated with virtue ethics, Aristotle, lived and taught even further back, over 1,000 years before the events of Karbala. Thus, one might justifiably ask, "To what extent can narratives from the past (such as Karbala) help inform our own moral impulses today?" Without doubt, if historical contexts shape virtues, then it is quite probable that the virtues of ancient Greek aristocrats such as Aristotle and his audience should not matter to us today. If that is the case, and if we throw out such culturally laden prejudices and priorities, then we might very well also throw out virtue ethics altogether. After all, we have derived virtue ethics from Aristotle's philosophy, as well as, by extension, his cultural-historical context.

Philosopher Martha Nussbaum, in response, argues that there are basic human drives and motivations held in common across times and cultures. Making her case, she considers the description of ancient Greeks who lived before Aristotle, those who "used to go around armed with swords," as outdated and uncivilized.[9] This image provides Nussbaum with an occasion to reflect on the possibility that some experiences are culturally bound, and thus culturally relative, while others are universal, including mortality, the body, pleasure and pain, cognitive capability, practical reason, early infant development, affiliation, and humor.[10] Universal virtues reflect our shared human experiences, even as we transform from a society that wields its swords in public to one that does not.[11] There are some universal human propensities that allow for the possibility of a virtue ethics that transcends the locality of any distinct cultural context. Nussbaum's conception of a universal virtue ethics, one that applies to modern life, would mean abstracting the most natural of human necessities from cultural contexts now quite strange and unfamiliar.

Nussbaum's argument about the virtues suggests the existence of a unifying human nature. As she elaborates elsewhere, Nussbaum draws on Aristotle's functional and realistic conception of human nature to address philosopher Bernard Williams (d. 2003).[12] Williams rejected (what he thought to be) Aristotle's idea that a fixed and externally identified human nature might somehow inform moral action, when motivations must come from within. Nussbaum argues that Aristotle's presentation of human nature focuses on the individual as well as those who are in community with them. An internal assessment of one's place in "life and action," one focused on experience, reveals human nature to each of us, instead of an external, perfect, and essential definition of such nature.[13] Aristotle is, in other words, concerned with defining human nature for those who belong to a community that might engage and interact with that person.[14] Rather than promoting a transformation into a wholly other person—becoming godlike through a complete transformation of character—Aristotle's ethics teaches its audience to focus on who they really are.[15] This puts Nussbaum's assessment of human nature at odds with models that do promote a radical or divine transformation of the self, such as in many Islamic philosophies.[16] Human nature, for Nussbaum, can certainly change over time, as communities grow and cultural norms shift. Nevertheless, on account of the grounding human experiences mentioned above, human nature will largely stay the same.[17] Through a reading of Aristotle, Nussbaum offers a community-focused human nature that is not blindly universal, even if it has some universal human qualities.

Nussbaum's argument aligns her with a select group of humanists and social scientists who persist in viewing humans in a more traditional way, as having some unifying nature. In recent times, their disciplines have frequently been overshadowed by theories emphasizing the cultural construction of knowledge and the absolute relativity of values. Such theories often imply a shift away from conceptions of a singular human nature, or even explicitly deny human universals. A notable figure in this regard is the anthropologist Clifford Geertz (d. 2006), who rejected the idea of a universal human nature. Geertz proposed that the diversity and distinctiveness of the world's disparate cultures might indicate a human "essence" more than any conception of one human nature.[18] In other words, what makes us different matters more than what we imagine makes us the same.

I raise this issue because, in the case of the warrior ethos, the wide scope of human norms seems to favor Geertz's skepticism over Nussbaum's more panoramic view of human sameness. After all, as we will see later in this book, there seems to be drastic cultural differences in the way societies express, receive, and even abandon the warrior ethos.

Perhaps a solution lies in applying Geertz's understanding of human cultural diversity to Nussbaum's adaptable model of human nature: Any claim about human universals must only come after having more than a basic understanding of the cultural practices and narratives we wish to include in our conversation—especially the practices and narratives of others. Let us begin, for example, with the image of all men "armed with swords," a practice that seems entirely absurd to Aristotle and—judging from Nussbaum's use—should ostensibly seem absurd to us as well. Aristotle comments that:

> In ancient times customs were exceedingly simple and barbaric: Greeks went about armed, and bought their brides from each other. Indeed the relics of ancient customs which are still in existence, here and there, are absurd.[19]

Yet the carrying of arms appears less culturally farfetched upon reading the passage where the historian Thucydides (d. ca. 398 BCE) describes this practice. He reports that the Greeks and the Barbarians, by which he seems to have meant the Phoenicians, Carians, and Epirotes, once lived lawlessly, engaging in piracy. The habitual carrying of swords by mainland Greeks is in fact "a survival of their old freebooting life."[20] He continues,

> Indeed, all the Hellenes used to carry arms because the places where they dwelt were unprotected, and intercourse with each other was unsafe; and in their everyday life they regularly went armed just as the Barbarians did. And the fact that these districts of Hellas still retain this custom is an evidence that at one time similar modes of life prevailed everywhere. But the Athenians were among the very first to lay aside their arms and, adopting an easier mode of life, to change to more luxurious ways.[21]

In such perilous situations, perhaps all of us would go around armed with swords. Without civil society, the virtuous thing to do—one might say—would be to remain vigilant, brave, and indeed armed. The rise of the city relieved the Greeks of the need for every man to be armed, wherein warfare became specialized and the various cities' inhabitants developed a sense of commonality that brought internal safety. This need not mean that the Greeks who carried arms lacked a cohesive system of virtues—or were uncivilized, even if one wants to argue that they lived in uncivilized times: They would have had little ability to change the relationships that they had with other tribes around them, at least not within a lifetime or part of a lifetime. Thus, their precarious relations with those around them were not so much a matter of character, as they were circumstance.

For Nussbaum, this mention of swords among the Greeks before Aristotle is meant to remind us that, even for Aristotle, there existed both an awareness of constant cultural change and "common features" or "grounding experiences" so that some rendition of virtue ethics could be cross-cultural.[22] Perhaps, however, even these changes—this process of urbanization and state formation—might be considered a "grounding experience," at least for those of us who live in contexts that have undergone this shift. Indeed, such changes in Greek society do not seem much different from the histories of most other city-dwelling people who were, at one time, tribal.

Perhaps, beyond what Nussbaum lists as grounding experiences of human nature, the development of civilizations has resulted in other common experiences: urbanization, the specialization of warlike virtues, and fundamental changes in virtues related to valor and conceptions of manhood. Those living in societies that have undergone this shift (namely, urbanized people, usually living in an expansive state) would then often struggle to see tribal virtues as virtues, especially when those virtues pertain to war, and this includes Aristotle. After all, even if Nussbaum is right and certain core grounding experiences seem not to change between human societies, most grounding experiences change with major shifts in a society's way of living—and can change quite significantly.

Bringing this closer to home, this book is premised on an idea that we might learn from an un-grounding experience. A cultural setting different from suburban America might enrich my life, not in spite of its tribal, warrior experiences, but because of them. Put differently, Nussbaum's argument works quite well when moral reasoning is limited to a certain sort of life, one sheltered from the wars in which our state engages or for which it offers support. Yet one wonders if even this sort of sheltered existence can benefit from remembering intentionally those who carried swords because of the constant threat of war—or those who still live in such precarities. Virtue tends to become even more valuable in times of urgency, conflict, difficult decisions, and abnormality, in fact, so it might be possible to learn an extreme variety of virtue from extreme circumstances.[23]

With all this in mind, the "universals" that comprise the virtues of this warrior narrative (namely, bravery, sincerity, self-worth, self-sacrifice, and loyalty) remain celebrated by those living the sheltered life. Less seemingly universal is the warrior's assumption of risk, which sometimes extends to a willingness to accept permanent injury or death. Those sheltered from war do indeed value the warrior's intrepid relationship with well-being, but usually without a sense of universality. Rather, we realize how much we lack it or have allegorized that ethos, rendering it something new that calls back upon that original warrior ethos but in a safer, even pacified way.

Historical Cultural Contexts of Islam's Warrior Ethos

In what setting did Islam's warrior ethos come to be? The earliest Arabic-language source on Islam, namely, the Quran, describes Muhammad and his followers as a communal army, formed to protect "houses in which God's name is often remembered," that is, "monasteries, churches, synagogues, and mosques."[24] The Quran asks its believers to combine their resources in protecting God's people and places from unbelievers.[25] Overwhelmingly, the Quran and the Hadith describe a collective spirit that locates felicity in a willingness to die for God's cause on the battlefield.[26]

One sees this warrior spirit in the recreational activities of early Muslims, which prepared them for the demands of war and included sprinting, horseback riding, swimming, archery, and wrestling, all of which emphasize martial skills.[27] One sees it also in the request of the Prophet's wife, ʿĀʾisha, to join in the armed efforts to protect monotheism (*jihad*): "I sought permission from the Prophet for jihad, and he replied, 'The jihad for you women is the Hajj.'"[28] That is, everyone—whether man or woman—was caught up in the spirit of martial altruism and wanted to take part in the armed defense of God's religion. Women seeking the felicity of self-sacrifice should, however, direct their efforts to the pilgrimage to Mecca and its environs. Both jihad and Hajj are variations on a common theme, namely, the willingness to give up comfort and safety in order to please God, but clearly there existed a sentiment that almost every able person should participate in armed combat.

Things had not always been this way for Muhammad and his followers. Muslim sacred sources tell us that the early community, living in Mecca, endured acts of torture and even murder for their beliefs, as well as a long and difficult embargo. They never fought back, at that early stage. Eventually, the Prophet Muhammad moved his persecuted community of monotheists to a city where they could try to worship in peace, a city now called Medina. There they established a functioning city-state, with laws and with an army.

For as long as anyone could remember, well before Muhammad's time, society had been tribal. There were settled tribes, who occupied the cities, and there were nomadic tribes. Some tribes were allied to each other, while others had longstanding feuds. Muhammad and his followers managed to accomplish two very important feats that would shape the area. First, they successfully spread the Quran's message of prophetic monotheism to many in the Arabian Peninsula. Second, they began to unite the tribes of the Arabian Peninsula, so that Medina became a capital to this confederacy of tribal alliances.[29] During Muhammad's lifetime, the Muslim community shifted its focus toward the lands of the Byzantine and Persian empires that surrounded them, lands such as the Levant, North Africa, Mesopotamia, and Persia. After his lifetime, they began to expand thereto: It was one of the most astonishing and important series of conquests in history, marking a major shift in the social and political structures of Western Asia.

As Muslim rule expanded during the period immediately following the life of Muhammad, what had been local and communal armies began to look more like an imperial army. The vast size of that army during the caliphate of ʿUmar (r. 634–644) meant that the organizational methods of his predecessors would not suffice, so that the caliph began to implement a register (*dīwān*) that helped disburse accumulated wealth among soldiers and others in the community.[30] The details of this shift remain somewhat obscure, but we do know that an elaborate system of payment for both Arab and non-Arab soldiers was in place by the time of the Umayyad caliphate, which began in 661 CE and lasted for almost a century.[31] Eventually, in this Muslim empire, there would come to be a distinction between citizens and soldiers. Later, large numbers of enslaved soldiers would come to characterize Islam's armies, beginning in the Abbasid period, over a hundred years after Muhammad's lifetime.

Yet this shift to large, imperial armies was not fully completed during al-Ḥusayn's lifetime, around sixty years after the Prophet settled in Medina. Still, in al-Ḥusayn's lifetime, serving as a warrior could be expected of most free men. While soldiers in al-Ḥusayn's time were rewarded, they were not always professionals. Al-Ḥusayn's supporters—like himself—represented a time like that of al-Ḥusayn's grandfather, the Prophet Muhammad, when all able-bodied men could be expected to carry swords.

Thus, al-Ḥusayn and his followers had inherited a warrior ethos from those before them. In pre-Islamic Arabia, the warrior ethos demanded loyalty to one's tribal elder.[32] In the Quran, this warrior ethos has acquired a devotional dimension, because the patron or master is God Himself. In other words, the warrior's love, loyalty, and sacrifice belong to God. God has loved those under His protection, and, in return, they "love Him."[33] This brings them to cultivate a propensity to sacrifice, giving of their wealth and even their lives.[34] God rewards them, in turn, with Paradise in the hereafter.[35]

Such sacrifice leads to the supreme felicity, as appears in "visitation prayers" for al-Ḥusayn in the Shiʿi tradition. One sees this in the "Visitation Prayer of Forty Days" ("Ziyārat al-Arbaʿīn"), which Shiʿi Muslims would ideally recite at al-Ḥusayn's shrine, in Karbala, forty days after the anniversary of his martyrdom. There, the pilgrim proclaims to al-Ḥusayn: "You lived in felicity, endured in praise, and died in bereavement and oppression, as a martyr."[36] The happy life, the life fully lived, is that of the martyr, because the successful conclusion of life is actually the fruition of years of preparation. Everything good in that person's life comes together to lead to a worthy death on the battlefield. Put differently, al-Ḥusayn's perfectly lived life has led to a perfectly executed death: one where he is praised, is bereaved, and has done no wrong to others, instead enduring oppression himself. It is with this in mind that the Shiʿi pilgrim also visits his shrine on the anniversary of his death, day of ʿĀshūrāʾ. On that day, the pilgrim recites a different formula of visitation and formally recognizes al-Ḥusayn's life and death as models of virtue in a manner like the Prophet Muhammad's were: "O God, make my life like the life of Muḥammad and his family, and make my death like the death of Muḥammad and his family."[37] Certainly, the battlefield is only one dimension of that life well-lived. Yet it is the dimension most telling of moral character, because it is on the battlefield that character shows itself most completely.

Discerning Virtue at Karbala

Like other virtues, the warrior ethos reveals itself most lucidly in narrative or, more specifically during moments when a decision is made, moments that reveal the moral reasoning of the agent making it. Such key moments do indeed appear in historical accounts of Karbala, even when terms for this warrior virtue do not. A sense of generosity, honesty, and self-worth permeates accounts describing the last stand of al-Ḥusayn or the events preceding or following that stand.

Without doubt, generosity, honesty, and self-worth number among the norms of battle applied to noble Arabian soldiers. These norms are so entrenched in the lifeways of al-Ḥusayn's era, that al-Ḥusayn can expect certain noble traits even from his callous enemy. Merely as Arabs, the enemies of al-Ḥusayn seem to be expected to abide by certain standards of nobility, despite their transgressions as Muslims, that is, despite their failure to observe the respect due to al-Ḥusayn, as the grandson of the Prophet. To give an example, as his own death looms, al-Ḥusayn notices a group of the enemy approaching his womenfolk and provisions. He calls out to them:

> Woe unto you! If you have no religion and you do not fear the Day of the Return, then at least—in your worldly affairs—be free men of noble traits. Safeguard my camp and and my family from the cruel and dissolute among you.[38]

The negative reply al-Ḥusayn receives, the refusal to guarantee safety for his womenfolk, underscores the ignoble natures of those who murdered him. They stand in contrast to the generosity and self-worth, or, more simply, "honor," that one could expect from a person of noble birth in Arabia, piety aside. "Free men" were, in the Arabian tradition of the time, those possessing noble qualities due to their descent. That is, a self-respecting Arab from a noble lineage would expect more from himself than to harm unarmed women, children, and other dependents. He would hold himself to a standard of clemency regarding the protected, the weak, and the bystander, just as he would hold himself to a standard of bravery regarding the strong, the armed, and the hostile.

As will be discussed in Chapter 2, the warrior ethos combines other virtues within the context, usually, of martial self-sacrifice. So, for example, one can see a combination of self-worth, loyalty, and courage appear quite evidently on the night before the massacre of al-Ḥusayn's troops. It is then that, as an act of generosity to his followers, al-Ḥusayn tells the men that they may leave, for "this night has provided a cover for you, so take it as a means to ride off, as if it were a camel."[39] His lifting of obligations is a sign of his generosity and hence nobility. His supporters' refusal to abandon him is a sign of their fortitude and hence nobility. Moreover, the responses he receives—a reaffirmation of their allegiances—indicates precisely the sort of self-worth that motivates the warrior's loyalty. Among those responses is that of Saʿd ibn ʿAbdallāh al-Ḥanafī, who declares:

> By God, we will not leave you all alone … By God, were I to know that I would be killed then brought to life, then burned alive, my ashes scattered, and that would happen seventy times, over and over, I would not part

> with you until I met my fate here at your service! How, then, could I not do this, when this means being killed only once? Moreover, it is a nobility (*al-karāma*) that will never expire.[40]

Sa῾d's sense of self-worth becomes expressed in his recognition of the value of his life: His body, his pain, and his experiences matter enough for him to be offering them. He has been overcome by loyalty, to the point that the sacrifice he makes seems simple, especially compared to the seventy deaths he is willing to suffer. He swears by God not only for emphasis but to underline his sincerity and his honesty.

The warrior's sense of loyalty becomes repeated by a more famous companion of al-Ḥusayn, Zuhayr ibn al-Qayn, who responds:

> By God, I would wish to be killed, then brought back, then killed, until I suffered one thousand such deaths, if it meant that God might prevent thereby your murder and the murder of these young men from your household.[41]

In like manner, al-Ḥusayn's agnate brother, al-῾Abbās ibn ῾Alī, declares his allegiance before losing his life in battle, defending his brother and chief:

> I do not fear death when death arises
> even if it means I face being buried among the sword-wielders.
> May my soul be protection for the pure one, who is as the Prophet's own soul.
> I am al-῾Abbās, who rushes to provide water to others.[42]

The "purity" of al-Ḥusayn, that is, his ethical impeccability, inspires his brother's bravery; moreover, the source of that purity is the Prophet Muhammad, whose virtues are reflected in his grandson, al-Ḥusayn.[43] Both Zuhayr and al-῾Abbās here touch on a major theme of the Karbala narratives, namely, the exalted status of the family of the Prophet. It becomes clear in these narratives that that status brings with it expectations of a set of ethical traits, which al-Ḥusayn models for his followers, traits that shine brightly in this moment of crisis, that is, the impending battle.

To that effect, one sees that al-Ḥusayn's presentation of his resistance is clearly one with a spotlight on some status inseparable from qualities that he shares with his close family, the family of the Prophet. That status must continuously befit the noble household that has received revelation. One notices it in the response he gives when asked by a representative of Yazīd to swear allegiance to the caliph:

> O emir! We are the People of the House of Prophecy, the mine of revelation, frequented by angels. Through us, God opens, and through us, God seals shut. Yazīd, however, is a transgressor, an imbiber of wine, murderer

> of the innocent, flagrant in his debauchery. Such stature does not belong to him. Someone like me cannot swear allegiance to someone like him. Yet we will greet the new day, just as you will greet the new day: We will wait and see, and you will wait and see, which of us is more deserving of the caliphate and of taking allegiances.[44]

It is particularly the phrase "someone like me" (*mithlī*) that gives us an appreciation for the set of traits that have driven al-Ḥusayn to becoming trapped in Karbala. The contrast between the way in which al-Ḥusayn sees himself—and knows the Muslim community to see him—and the way in which he and others see Yazīd ("someone like him") influences the major decisions in this narrative.

While this report does not appear in al-Ṭabarī, another similar one does: Facing coercion to declare his allegiance to Yazīd, al-Ḥusayn tells al-Walīd and Marwān, relatives and supporters of Yazīd, that the timing and situation of this request is unsuitable. "Concerning this allegiance that you ask me to swear," al-Ḥusayn says, "secret allegiances do not suit someone like me."[45] The allegiance must be public, for someone of al-Ḥusayn's importance. While somewhat different, both of the above quotations stress that al-Ḥusayn's lineage and character elevate him beyond being a solitary or ordinary man. He embodies a category of humanity, an elite moral type, as expressed in the phrase used in both quotations, "someone like me." He is a paragon, a moral leader, and widely considered worthy of imitation. Again, his status seems to be both the source and the major factor of influence in his moral actions.

Moral Reasoning of the Noble Warrior

In the domain of making choices, the warrior has certain expectations of himself that not only help clarify things but also lead to selfless acts, such as those we have seen above. Mohammad Jafar Amir Mahallati has considered the relationship between Karbala and the living Shiʿi ethical tradition. Mahallati indicates ways in which that narrative has affected Shiʿi legal views, such as in its prohibition of terrorism, pointing specifically to the eminent twentieth-century Shiʿi jurist, Ḥusayn-ʿAlī Muntaẓirī. The warrior ethos, as conveyed by the Karbala narrative, can help clarify the proper moral attitude toward using violence for a greater good. Is all really fair in war? The warrior ethos suggests that the answer to that is "no."

To understand the gravity of the decision made and to appreciate the "greater good" that might have resulted from one act of violence, the reader will need some background: Before the Battle of Karbala, al-Ḥusayn had been invited by the people of Kufa, Iraq, to move there from his home in Medina and become their leader and governor. His father, ʿAlī, had taken Kufa as his center of rule while he was caliph, so it was a natural destination for him. To test the seriousness of their promises of support, al-Ḥusayn sent his cousin Muslim ibn ʿAqīl there.

It turned out that their invitations to al-Ḥusayn had been empty promises. Once a new governor took over and established draconian intimidation tactics, the people of Kufa became subdued by fear. That governor, ʿUbaydallāh ibn Ziyād, would later dictate the murder of al-Ḥusayn in Karbala. At a certain point, while he was in Kufa, al-Ḥusayn's cousin, Muslim ibn ʿAqīl, had an opportunity to kill the governor furtively. This occurred when Muslim visited the house of Hāniʾ ibn ʿUrwa, in which he was hiding. Yet he did not, and in not doing so cited a statement of the Prophet in support of his actions.[46]

Indeed, when asked why he failed to take advantage of this opportunity, one that would have prevented the murder of al-Ḥusayn and countless others, including that of himself and his sons, Muslim's response pointed to the virtues of a warrior ethos:

> Two things [prevented me from killing him]. The first is that Hāniʾ hated for [ʿUbaydallāh] to be killed in his home. The second is a saying that people have reported from the Prophet, "Belief [in God] keeps one from committing murder in ambush. The believer never kills furtively."[47]

One should not be misled by the first point, namely that his host (named Hāniʾ) did not want the murder to happen in his home. Hāniʾ knew that the governor, ʿUbaydallāh, deserved to die. In fact, despite Hāniʾ's feelings of hospitality, the governor would later have Hāniʾ executed. The issue for Hāniʾ was in the location of the potential murder, "for," Hāniʾ himself says, "you would have killed a transgressor, a profligate, a stubborn opponent of God, and a betrayer, but I did indeed hate for him to be killed in my home."[48] Hāniʾ felt so bound by expectations of hospitality that he simply could not bear for the murder to take place while ʿUbaydallāh was his guest.

Phrased differently, we might say that Hāniʾ abided by the *virtue* of hospitality, that is, his idealized expectation of what one might expect from a host (in a premodern Arabian context). In like manner, Muslim ibn ʿAqīl attributed the second reason to something within himself: In refraining from murdering the governor furtively, he abided by the virtue of the noble warrior. In this, Muslim relied on a report of the Prophet. At first glance, this report might be understood as a Kantian universal: One must never kill furtively. Yet, as a believer and warrior, Muslim did clearly struggle with the decision and initially planned to ambush the governor, so it does not seem to be a universal rule. Moreover, the language of the report indicates that his moral reasoning has relied instead on a series of expectations that one might have of the "believer" in a warlike or hostile setting. One might, in fact, translate the Prophet's saying as "Furtive killing does not befit the believer." It is, after all, an act of cowardice and thus a shameful act. In this, we see that the Karbala narrative, for which Muslim's last days in Kufa were a prelude, captures those characteristics that historians such as al-Ṭabarī might have expected from the ideal warrior, the same characteristics of which al-Ḥusayn's enemies were bereft.

One might compare the warrior values at work here, and the way that they might be in danger of being simplified as moral law, to Jeff Mitchell's description of the Roman virtue of *honestum* (a sort of "honorable propriety") according to Cicero. Cicero's description of this duty might be misinterpreted by a contemporary audience, for in a "post-Kantian age, the idea of duty is almost inevitably interpreted as being based upon a moral law or principle."[49] Yet, rather than being rule-based, the virtue was a reflection of what he and others came to expect of the reasonable gentleman, rather, the often unspoken "moral sensibility" of ruling elites.[50] Here moral reasoning was also of a ruling minority, warriors for whom honesty, bravery, and hospitality had become informed by God-consciousness, for they were now God's warriors. Their moral model was that of the Arabian prophet and the larger tribal family to which he belonged, the Quraysh, who shared a set of virtues from pre-Islamic martial history, which had become—from their perspective—enhanced and perfected when expounded in revelation. Al-Ḥusayn embodied such virtues.

Conclusion

This chapter has illustrated how a certain virtue can be abstracted from a historical battle narrative. So far, I have referred to this as a "warrior ethos." In Chapter 2 we will discover why "warrior nobility" is a more precise way to envision this ethos within the context of Islam. "Warrior nobility" has been and remains an integral virtue within Muslim lifeways.

Notes

1 As Aun Hasan Ali discusses, the affective aspect of commemorating Karbala must be considered a major component, one independently significant in that it is not contingent on such remembrance's ethical concerns. See Ali (2014).
2 Jaʿfarīyān (2003 [1382 SH], 87). See also Ansari (2010a, 2010b).
3 Robinson (2003, 25).
4 It should be noted that these devotional communities would say that they have *discerned* or *discovered* dimensions of meaning within this event—an important distinction.
5 Jan Assmann labels "mnemohistory" that which investigates "the history of cultural memory," namely, the ways in which texts form a coherent narrative—an act of interpretation practiced by poets and scholars alike, even if the mythical elements in poetry externalize the process of narrativity more manifestly than the feigned objectivity of historians. See Assmann, *Moses the Egyptian*, pp. 15–16.
6 Wellhausen (1975, 112).
7 MacIntyre (2007, 208).
8 Anscombe (1958, 176).
9 Nussbaum (1988, 32).
10 Nussbaum (1988, 48–49).
11 Nussbaum (1988, 46); see also Russell (2009, 173–174).

12 Nussbaum (1995, 89).
13 Nussbaum (1995, 94, 102).
14 Nussbaum (1995, 106, 108–109).
15 Nussbaum (1995, 91).
16 Faruque (2021, 259–260).
17 Nussbaum (1995, 120–121). In Paul Woodruff's reading of Aristotle (and, in part, his reading of Nussbaum's interpretation of Aristotle), humans, as a whole, "gravitate" in a certain direction—one that includes the formation of cities. See Woodruff (1991, 332).
18 Geertz (1973, 45).
19 Aristotle (1995, 2.8, 1268b22, p. 65).
20 Thucydides (1956, Book I. V. 2-vi, p. 11).
21 Thucydides (1956, Book I. V. 2-vi, p. 11).
22 Nussbaum (1988, 46); see also Russell (2009, 173–174).
23 As we will explore later in this book, moreover, if social context can change a human being so fundamentally that war and conflict become matters private to ruling technocrats, carried out by the poorest citizens, as well as robotic drones, then it might be safe to say that a distinct variety of cowardice and large-scale warfare are in fact two sides of one modern moral coin.
24 Quran 22:40.
25 Quran 9:111.
26 Quran 9:36.
27 al-Suyūṭī (1992).
28 al-Bukhārī (2002, 710, no. 2875).
29 Donner (1981, 267–273).
30 Hodgson (1974, 1:208).
31 Crone (2003).
32 Indeed, Toshihiko Izutsu has shown how the Quran adopts and alters older Arabian virtues, converting them into monotheistic ones suited to the mission of Muhammad. See Izutsu (2002), *Ethico-Religious Concepts in the Qur'ān*.
33 Quran 5:54.
34 Quran 9:44 and 9:81.
35 Quran 9:111.
36 Qummī (1997, 593).
37 Qummī (1997, 582).
38 al-Ṭabarī (2008, 5:304).
39 al-Ṭabarī (2008, 5:283).
40 al-Ṭabarī (2008, 5:283).
41 al-Ṭabarī (2008, 5:283).
42 al-Mawlā'ī (2005, 4:402).
43 While al-Ḥusayn and al-ʿAbbās share the same father, they do not share the same mother—Fāṭima—who is the Prophet's daughter; hence, only al-Ḥusayn is the Prophet's grandson. Al-ʿAbbās makes a similar statement in two double lines (*bayt*s), the first of which will be quoted in Chapter 3: "By God, even if they cut off my right arm / I will zealously protect my religion (*dīnī*) with perseverance (*ṣābiran*) / as well as an imam, truthful in certainty, / from the progeny of the Prophet, pure and trustworthy." See al-Muqarram (2012, 275).
44 Ibn Ṭāwūs (1998, 42).
45 al-Ṭabarī (2008, 5:228).
46 Mahallati (2016, 176).
47 al-Ṭabarī (2008, 5:245).
48 al-Ṭabarī (2008, 5:245).
49 Mitchell (2019, 98).
50 Mitchell (2019, 98–99).

2 Noblest among Us

The Comprehensive Virtue of *Karam*

To Muslim ethicists, "nobility" encapsulates other virtues, and Karbala exemplifies nobility to a degree arguably unmatched by any other event in the history of Islam after the time of the Prophet. Since the first of commentators began writing about al-Ḥusayn and his followers, Muslim writers have remained well aware of a constellation of virtues that they associate with the warrior, on full display in the Karbala narrative. For them, the battlefield serves as a place of realization for the virtues one has cultivated throughout life. They tend to identify "nobility," or *karam* in Arabic, as the sum of those virtues. For that reason, I focus on *karam* or nobility, even though the reader should be aware of other somewhat similar virtues in Arabic literature, particularly those that were more common among Arabic speakers before Islam.

One term that indicated praiseworthy preeminence was *ʿirḍ*, or "honor," indicating power and achievement. This term does not appear in the Quran and hence has a marginal role in Islamic ethics. There is also *sharaf*, meaning "preeminence," often meaning that one is highborn, but rarely associated with ethical achievement on the scale of *karam*. More significant would be the term *murūʾa*, or "manliness," which—like the aforementioned word *futuwwa* ("youngmanliness")—can signify a kind of chivalry. Before Islam, as the historian of Islam Ignaz Goldziher describes it, Arabian society valued reputation, respect for family relations, hospitality, loyalty, self-sacrifice, and the protection of those in one's care. These traits comprised the virtue of manliness.[1] Expectations of manliness called for revenge when one's tribe or wards were wronged. Islam's emphasis on forgiveness, patience, and leniency altered the definition of this virtue.[2] Yet, even though its new form allowed manliness to remain an important virtue in Islamic literature, manliness did not find its way into the Quran, which shows a preference for *karam* as the centerpiece of human praiseworthiness. Moreover, in texts that outline al-Ḥusayn's virtues, *karam* clearly has pride of place.

Works that might be called "ethical biographies" illustrate to us how *karam* has been a comprehensive and even chief Islamic virtue. A notable example is Kamāl al-Dīn ibn Ṭalḥa al-Shāfiʿī (d. 1254), a Sunni scholar with a special allegiance to the twelve Shiʿi imams. In his book on the virtues of

DOI: 10.4324/9781003265191-3

the Prophet's family, al-Shāfiʿī describes al-Ḥusayn as the full achievement of praiseworthy characteristics:

> It is well-known and widely narrated that he [al-Ḥusayn], God's blessings be upon him, honored his guests, granted the needs of seekers, observed the bonds of kinship, helped the poor, served the petitioner, clothed the naked, fed the hungry, gave to the one in debt, supported the weak, commiserated with the orphan, aided the one in trouble, and rarely did any wealth come to him but that it parted quickly from him.[3]

One might summarize al-Shāfiʿī's description by saying, "al-Ḥusayn was noble," but the author wants to elaborate not only on instantiations of al-Ḥusayn's nobility but also on the acts that might be expected from a noble person, acts of hospitality, family loyalty, service, self-sacrifice, and generosity.

The Shiʿi historian Abū al-Ḥasan ʿAlī ibn ʿĪsā ibn Abī al-Fatḥ al-Irbīlī (d. ca. 1293) clarifies the relationship of these virtues to "nobility," in a passage on al-Ḥusayn. He makes three important points. First, Irbīlī establishes that nobility (*al-karam*) is a compound virtue, or in his words, "nobility (*al-karam*) is a comprehensive word for all praiseworthy traits." Its corresponding vice is "vileness" (*al-luʾm*), "which is the comprehensive word for all evil traits." Second, nobility becomes known through modeling, that is, it only becomes apparent when seen practiced by noble individuals, even if others have a sense of the virtues that make it up before they see it in its fullest expression. Particularly, people appreciate "liberality" (*al-jūd*) as the visible social manifestation of nobility, because we intuitively appreciate giving, generosity, and self-sacrifice, and recognize it as an indicator of other virtues. Third and last, those "for whom nobility was firmly established, in whom it was realized, and to whom it was assigned in a particular way" were none other than the family of the Prophet Muhammad. Their actions and words always showed nobility. Indeed, as the author states, "they [the Prophet and his family] were its full reality, so that nobility was only metaphorical for everyone else."[4] It is from nobility that upright actions emanate, and this quality is especially strong in the Prophet Muhammad's family, according to these authors. Nobility becomes the virtue par excellence that describes al-Ḥusayn, his actions, and his sacred prophetic lineage. That others can never wholly achieve nobility in the way that the Prophet and his family do seems to be a recognition of what I will discuss in Chapter 4 as "factitious virtues."

To explain, the relationship between al-Ḥusayn's legendary actions and nobility involves more than his own personal nobility. It includes his entire family. Indeed, al-Ḥusayn was predisposed to nobility through his descent from the Prophet, a nobility that al-Ḥusayn cultivated within his own life. The effects of that nobility are the other virtues, which result in his actions at Karbala, virtues such as bravery. Ibn Ṭalḥa's concern with establishing al-Ḥusayn's nobility brings the author, for example, to continue for two pages to recount the unparalleled bravery of al-Ḥusayn, since al-Ḥusayn's bravery bears witness to his nobility. According to Ibn Ṭalḥa, just as al-Ḥusayn's nobility causes his bravery, so too does his bravery cause heroic action.[5] That action was largely an act of rejecting the authority of a tyrannical caliph, despite the threat of certain death. Such bravery also appeared in al-Ḥusayn's continued refusal to capitulate, even when faced with a large army of "traitors" who had once "broken their allegiance," now loyal to the governor of Kufa and to that governor's superior, the caliph Yazid.[6] In contrast to that army's massive size was the paucity of al-Ḥusayn's own loyal forces, which included young men dear to him, many related to him by blood, whose defeat would leave his womenfolk and children exposed.[7] "Despite all this," Ibn Ṭalḥa says, al-Ḥusayn was "firm, his bravery lacking even an iota of fear, and his gallant resolve lacking all timidity as well, for his footing was firmer than the mountains."[8]

Of interest here is that this description crescendos until Ibn Ṭalḥa can quote al-Ḥusayn's own lines of battle poetry, proclaimed on the day of his martyrdom. It was common in this period for warriors to recite a sort of battle poetry in the *rajaz* meter, often a variety called *fakhr*, or "glory poetry":[9]

> I am the son of ʿAlī, the greatest of the tribe of Hāshim;
> that suffices for me in terms of material for boasting.
> My grandfather was God's messenger, the most noble of those who have walked the earth.
> We are the Lantern of God, illuminating humankind.
> Fatima is my mother, from the line of the most praised one, Muhammad.
> My uncle, Jaʿfar, lays claim to being dubbed "the martyr who soars in Paradise with two wings."[10]

This discussion leads immediately to an exposition on nobility (*karam*), the very exposition quoted above and quoted by other authors on ethics, such as Mullā Muḥsin Fayḍ al-Kāshānī, in his later commentary on Abū Ḥāmid al-Ghazālī's *Revival of the Religious Sciences* (*Iḥyāʾ ʿUlūm al-Dīn*).[11] Yet one notices even here the emphasis on the nobility of al-Ḥusayn's forebears. Muslims could expect the grandson of their prophet to be brave, and it is in response to such expectations that he makes his final stand. Ibn Ṭalḥa, al-Irbīlī, and al-Kāshānī all build a case that al-Ḥusayn is the exemplar of nobility, or *karam*. The actions attributed to al-Ḥusayn describe a noble man (*karīm*) who behaves according to the highest standards of his community, indeed, whose actions set such standards.

Of course, as a descriptor, nobility does not exhaust al-Ḥusayn's ethical impulse at Karbala. Much of the language surrounding the sacrifices of al-Ḥusayn, his family, and his companions concerns complete resignation with God's will, a virtue called "satisfaction" (*riḍā*), or, perhaps even more frequently, love (*ḥubb*, *maḥabba*, or *ʿishq*). For example, the South Asian philosopher Muhammad Iqbal drew on Karbala to expound his theory of *khūdī*, or the idealized self.[12] Love, according to Iqbal, represents the underlying power of faith, one that outdoes reasoning. The "imam of lovers" is al-Ḥusayn, who channels the devotional and cosmic love made manifest by his father, ʿAlī, and mother, Fāṭima.[13] Iqbal's reading of al-Ḥusayn's borrows from his Sunni Sufi background and training to present him as a realization of true monotheistic love, so that no finer affirmation of being enamored by God's oneness exists than the statement by action al-Ḥusayn made when he "writhed in dust and blood."[14] In Karbala, Iqbal found an ideal model for the God-conscious pursuit of justice through love.[15] For Iqbal, the spirit of sacrifice in al-Ḥusayn's movement realized the superiority of love and knowledge to worldly power and wealth, which was an especially provocative message in the twentieth century, when so many Muslim intellectuals contemplated Marxist concerns with the economically underprivileged.[16]

Iqbal's analysis is not uncommon among Muslim interpretations of Karbala: Love is arguably the most salient theme of the poetry and storytelling that recounts the heroism of al-Ḥusayn and his followers. This indicates the degree to which any one discussion of the ethics of Karbala—including this discussion that focuses on nobility—will fall short in conveying the complexity of its moral legacy.

Nobility as Comprehensive Virtue

From a theoretical perspective, an idea hides behind the discussions of nobility as a comprehensive virtue, as a composite description that takes shape through the Arabian and Islamic cultural context of al-Ḥusayn's life. That is, in virtue ethics, there has long been a perspective that all virtues might be traced to one source virtue, even identified as facets of that one virtue. Socrates argued that that virtue was "wisdom," with the other virtues as constituent parts of one overarching virtue.[17] Later, with the rise of Christianity, Augustine would argue that one virtue could be identified as the reality of all other virtues. That virtue, for Augustine, was Christlike love.[18] The later Christian theologian Thomas Aquinas, however, followed Aristotle in seeing the virtues as interconnected only in a loose way, in that one can expect a virtuous person to possess all the virtues as long as that person exhibits the master virtue in question.[19]

To further appreciate how nobility might be a comprehensive virtue in its Islamic context, we might further consider efforts in Christian ethics to uncover a single origin for all virtuous character traits. Augustine saw all the virtues as one whole, although his position created another problem. The unity of virtue implied the unity of vice, which would seem to support the Stoic theory that all sins are equal. To Augustine, one is indeed guilty of all sins by committing just one sin, but that does not mean that every sin is equal: While the guilt of sin is one burden, the sins do differ in terms of gravity.

Yet the virtues are one because the virtuous person—in each expression of virtue—will naturally possess all the virtues at once. Augustine says that "he who has one virtue has them all, and he who does not have a particular one has none."[20] If a person lacks any of the virtues, in other words, then the virtues we might perceive (when a person is, for example, brave but not temperate) only resemble virtues: The person simulates a virtue in their actions.[21] Clearly, Augustine's notion of the unity of virtues and the pervasiveness of vice reflect his theological commitments. The first—the unity of good—corresponds to an ethical dimension of his Neoplatonic view of reality, the emanation of one good. The second—that any vice means a complete lack of all virtues—supports his position on original sin, namely, the idea that humanity has a fallen nature resulting from the first sin of Adam and Eve and remedied by Christ. That the highest good is God, and that the virtue behind all virtues is the love of God, has doubtless had a formative effect on much of Christian ethics.

In an analogous way, the Islamic interpretation of the Arabian virtue of nobility carries deep theological significance. Nobility, as portrayed in the Quran, is an ethical expression of God's oneness. After all, God is a singular supreme deity, but becomes known through multiple beautiful names, which are a series of descriptors found throughout the Quran and Islamic piety. From these descriptors, believers form their conception of God. From these descriptors, believers also form their conception of moral goodness. The human virtues reflect those names and are thus manifold realizations of God as the source of beautiful perfection. In this case, the believers strive for the virtue of nobility, and the Prophet Muhammad is "noble," yet it is God who is "most noble." Nobility is known most perfectly in God. Nobility seems to be a pivotal attribute, moreover, since, in one of the first verses of the Quran ever revealed, God introduces Himself as "the most noble."[22]

Moreover, the Quranic word *karīm*, or "noble," constantly depends on God's presence. On the one hand, *karīm* can mean "honored," such as in an "honored messenger."[23] Here none other than God determined that the messenger in question deserved honor. (The honored messenger in this instance is Moses, by the way.) On the other hand, *karīm* can mean "generous," such as in a "generous award."[24] Again, none other than God determines and gives that award. Indeed, God's gaze pervades every instance of nobility, whether as honor or as an instance of generosity. God always determines who deserves honor and, in doing so, indicates who is good. Thus, to be "honored" is to be "good." The expression of such noble goodness lies in generosity. A noble person will naturally want to give, for they possess a Godlike quality. As the most noble, God is also the most generous, for all things subject to generosity have their origins in a deity who created humans and provides for them "from the sky and the earth."[25]

The idea that the divine gaze lends ethical substance to nobility informs one particular verse especially. In that verse, the Quran describes the highest good as being cognizant of God's constant evaluation of human states and actions:

> O humans! We have created you male and female and rendered you as nations and tribes, in order that you might know one another. The most noble (*akramakum*) among you—to God—is the most Godwary of you. Indeed, God is the knowing, the aware.[26]

True nobility lies in perpetual mindfulness of God as "the aware" or "All-aware." Such mutual awareness (the believer's awareness of God's all-awareness) qualifies the believer for God's highest honor. That honor belongs to those who, through such awareness of God, adopt a God-aware approach to everything and thus a divinely sanctioned life. Constant awareness of God means constant reorientation toward the Ultimate Reality (*al-Ḥaqq*), whose beautiful names are the source of all things good.

This helps us understand al-Ḥusayn's expressions of Islamic nobility as acts unified by an awareness of God. Indeed, many of his statements in the Karbala narrative reveal an interrelationship between nobility and awareness of God's presence. Hence, when al-Ḥusayn sets out toward Mecca, he quotes a passage from the Quran describing the Biblical and Quranic hero, the prophet Moses: "So he [Moses] left from there, fearing and watching on guard. He said, 'My Lord, rescue me from this oppressive people.'"[27] As embodiments of God's nobility, figures such as al-Ḥusayn and Moses will be enemies to oppressors. Their undaunted defiance of the aims of oppressors stems from their alignment with what God loves and disdain for what God does not love, for "God does not love the oppressors."[28] Moreover, even when those oppressors seem free to kill or compel the noble, the noble remain aware of God's ability to alter everything and rescue them at any moment.[29]

Once again, when entering Mecca, al-Ḥusayn exhibits a nobility that comes from being aware of God. There he says, quoting the same passage about Moses in the Quran, "When he stood facing Midian, he [Moses] said, 'Perhaps my Lord will guide me to the proper way.'"[30] Here too, despite the odds against him, al-Ḥusayn shows awareness that God can improve his situation, even when He chooses not to. Yet, at the same time, al-Ḥusayn shows resignation and even satisfaction with this state of affairs, for being aware of God's presence means being aware of the wisdom behind what God determines.[31] This satisfaction defines al-Ḥusayn's nobility as exemplary.

One sees the satisfaction with God's decree indicative of nobility in the case of al-Ḥusayn's sister Zaynab as well. When held captive at the court of the governor who had planned and executed the murder of her brother, that governor—ʿUbaydallāh ibn Ziyād—asked her, in a demeaning way, "What do you think of what God has done to your brother and your family?" He intended, in this, to imply that God had willed and hence approved of the events as they unfolded. Her response has become famous in Shiʿi devotional circles: "I saw nothing but beauty."[32] She then proceeds to remind him that death is not the end of things: God's judgment awaits her family, as well as the governor, which does not bode well for him. Yet her response, the embracing of the horrific murder of her brothers, nephews, and even sons as "beauty," reveals that her perspective is a moral one. She sees the praiseworthy character traits on display in their final acts of heroism, character traits that reflect God's endless beauty. They died in a state of being pleased with God's command, so that God was pleased with them, a state called "satisfaction" (*riḍā*), associated in the Quran with life in Paradise.[33] Zaynab reflects such "satisfaction" in her interpretation of the events.

Zaynab is the female counterpart to the noble warrior, continuing the selfless struggle after the male warriors have been killed. One contemporary poet refers to her as "the source of knowledge," "the patient one," "the source of bravery," "the light of the universe," and even "the lioness of Karbala."[34] This combination of virtues points to the idea that, in a unified way, she realizes all forms of moral goodness. As with her brother, al-Ḥusayn, Zaynab's nobility derives from her family: Her grandfather, the Prophet, as well as her father, ʿAlī, her brothers, but especially her mother, Fāṭima.[35] This indicates that the English word "nobility," which derives from a Latin word meaning "highborn," might be a fitting translation for the *karam* she represents, a *karam* epitomized by Islam's spiritual elites, who serve as models for the Muslim community.

Warrior Nobility in Contemporary Rituals

One cannot consider the "warrior nobility" embodied in the Karbala narrative without also considering the cultural practices that convey both the narrative and its associated virtues. Indeed, Karbala first drew my attention—as it does for many—not through reading books of history but through watching ritual practices immortalizing the actions of al-Ḥusayn, his family, and his companions. The recitation of poetry, the recounting of events in story form, the sung chants accompanied by a crowd beating their chests, the serving of certain foods, and the decoration of religious spaces in colors and calligraphies of mourning: Karbala comes to life for most through cultural practices that heighten at the yearly anniversary of the event in the month of Muḥarram, as well as the fortieth-day anniversary of that event in the month following. Kamran Scot Aghaie gives the name "the Karbala Paradigm" to a series of cultural practices and symbols that draw on the Karbala narrative.[36] The most important and enduring quality of this paradigm is its conveyance of virtues and vices: al-Ḥusayn, his followers, and his family represent paragons of sacrifice and nobility, while his enemies represent the basest of human attributes. Practices such as Karbala morality plays (*taʿziyya*) or emotive recitation of the Karbala narrative (*rawḍa-khānī*), as well as a number of symbols in the narrative, have become completely infused with moral associations

Aghaie's focus is on the Karbala Paradigm specifically inside Iran and hence in Persian, but his observations can be applied to many of the places and languages in which al-Ḥusayn's actions endure through ritualized remembrance. For Iranians, argues Aghaie, the Karbala Paradigm has been a case of moral independence for those ruled by the state and by aristocrats, what we might call "morality from below." Despite waves of augmented significations—such as state-driven nationalism, anti-imperialist interpretations, and ideological apologetics—the central moral component of the Karbala Paradigm remains constant. Cultural practices and symbols have been so strongly associated with the Karbala Paradigm, that the associations have stood the test of time over centuries and major changes in Iran's government, from the Qajar monarchs of the nineteenth centuries to the Islamic Republic of today.

The transformative potential of remembering Karbala seems to be both moral and social, such that Babak Rahimi has considered ways in which Karbala rituals have a "carnivalesque" quality, referring to the phenomenon wherein gatherings, processions, and public rituals subvert the social order.[37] Rahimi argues that the body—in its blood, tears, and self-flagellation—allows for spaces of ambiguity, where social roles can be leveled and human impulses explored without being bound by determined (or even dogmatic) definitions.[38] This holds true for Karbala rituals both today and in Iran's Safavid past.

Ethical change is, in fact, a common theme in studies of Karbala rituals, regardless of place or culture. In the South Asian context, focusing on Hyderabad, India, Karen Ruffle has taken an interest in the practice of *mātam* ("self-flagellation"). She locates, in these practices, a nurturing, caring expression of masculinity. This is especially pronounced in the case of al-ʿAbbās, agnate brother to al-Ḥusayn, who brings together the "valiant" and yet also "softer" masculinities described by Amanullah De Sondy in his study of Islamic masculinities.[39] Devotional poetry and other recitals designate al-ʿAbbās as a caretaker, famously killed while bringing water back for the thirsty children in al-Ḥusayn's camp.[40]

In the Arabic context of Syria, Edith Szanto has studied the transformative potential of the remembrance of al-Ḥusayn, his sister Zaynab, and the Karbala narrative. According to Szanto, the language, representations, and rituals practiced during Muḥarram processions take on two modes, sometimes even within the same circle of mourners. The first (*athara*) is proper instruction about the legacy of this narrative or, one might say, the ethical impulse. The second (*thāra*) is movement toward action, one might say the revolutionary impulse.[41] These studies expand the scope of *karam* or nobility to include interpretations of moral well-being that matter in contemporary contexts. As a comprehensive virtue nobility expands—by its very nature—to include what interpreters deem to be upstanding qualities. They identify those qualities in the model of Islam's moral elites, namely, the Prophet's family.

Nobility of the Saint

To speak of the Prophet's household in Islam, especially in Shiʿi Islam, as merely "moral elites" would be enough of an understatement to qualify as a misstatement, especially if the larger theological significance of their status remained unmentioned. It is not a central concern here, because of my specific focus on Islam's warrior nobility from the perspective of virtue ethics. Yet it matters. The theological status of the Prophet's family pervades living and recorded accounts of al-Ḥusayn. In some ways, it is the most significant element in remembering Karbala as a tragedy, for the martyr killed gruesomely and unjustly in Karbala was the saintliest, purest, and worthiest leader of his time, from this theological perspective.

Much of this has been outlined elegantly by Karen Ruffle, in her study on the remembrance of Karbala in South Asia, *Gender, Sainthood, and Everyday Practice in South Asian Shiʿism.* Ruffle considers the way in which the "Ḥusaynī ethic" that encompasses sacrifice and faith, a function of the general sainthood (*wilāya*) of the Prophet and his family, includes authentic female voices and figures, celebrated for their femininity, especially but not exclusively al-Ḥusayn's mother, Fāṭima.[42] As Ruffle notes, the theological status of the Prophet and his family corresponds to a special sainthood called *walāya*, which is distinct but related to *wilāya*. The term *walāya* indicates their divine appointment in terms of knowledge, nearness to God, salvation, and service as moral models to humanity.[43] Ruffle's work builds on the study of sainthood in Moroccan Sufism by Vincent Cornell, in which Cornell overviews longstanding disagreements about the two terms, *wilāya* and *walāya*, maintained both inside Islam—by Sufis and others—and by non-Muslim specialists.[44]

Pertinent to Karbala, Cornell also argues that sainthood must always be a "discourse." In other words, sainthood must be recognized to be actualized, and it is recognized via miracles, hagiographies, intercession, accounts of piety, and memorable acts.[45] When that recognition becomes written, or even part of a literary or historical canon, that saint becomes what Cornell calls a "literary monument," building on Michel Foucault's idea that a collection of statements might become a "discursive formation."[46] This matters here because al-Ḥusayn's legacy, his ritualized, remembered, and recorded sainthood, contains within it multiple such monuments. There are enough discursive formations or saintly literary monuments in the account of al-Ḥusayn to qualify Karbala remembrance as its own mode of practice and writing, comprising multiple rituals and genres. Focusing only on saintly monuments, these include the sainthoods of his sister Zaynab, his brother al-ʿAbbās, his sons and daughters, his other family members, and his companions, their wives, and their children.

Yet this seeming multiplicity of monuments becomes united by certain thematic virtues, most especially love and nobility. One sees this, for example, in the many "visitation treatises" (*al-ziyārāt*) for each of these saints, which a person might recite at their shrine, or from far away, whether on a special day devoted to that saint, or often on any important day of the sacred calendar. Each of those visitation treatises tends to focus on two major themes: first, the relationship of the saint in question to the Prophet and his family. Thus, the visitation will begin with wishes of peace, addressing that saint as "daughter of God's messenger" or "helpers of Fāṭima, lady of all the women of all the worlds." Second, the visitation will contemplate the moral success of that saint, in enduring hardships for the sake of God and in dying nobly:

> You acted in a lovely way and made lovely the earth in which you were buried. You triumphed, by God, with a tremendous triumph. Woe is me! Had I only been with you so that I too might have triumphed with you in the gardens.[47]

The emphasis on triumph, emphasized by swearing in God's name, is perhaps the most interesting phenomenon—as seen here and in other visitation treatises. The triumph is a moral one: While the martyr has been killed and the battle has been lost in an earthly sense, it matters little, since the warrior has acted perfectly and achieved his full potential as a human being. This manifestation of human perfection has lingering effects, yielding not only the pleasure of God and the constant remembrance of believers through visitation but also the sanctification of the earth in which the martyr is buried. That earth becomes holy and lovely—and visitors to Karbala have, for centuries, brought small tablets of clay from Karbala to use during the prostrations of their ritual prayers. It is an accepted fact among Shiʿi Muslims that the earth of Karbala has curative properties and a pleasant fragrance.

The Gentleman Warrior: Between Unyieldingness and Love

The "nobility" element in warrior nobility has received sufficient attention. What about, however, the "warrior" element? Warrior nobility is a manifestation of nobility that appears in times of struggle and conflict, and not necessarily armed conflict. The Quran captures its parameters succinctly in the following verse:

> Muhammad is the messenger of God. Those with him are unyielding toward the hostile truth-coverers, merciful among themselves. You will see them bowing, prostrating, seeking grace from God—and His satisfaction. Their mark is on their foreheads, imprinted by prostration. That is their representation in the Torah, and their representation in the Gospel is as a young crop the shoot of which comes out, so that it thickens and straightens at its stalk, delighting the farmers—so that, through them, He

> might enrage the hostile truth-coverers. God has promised forgiveness to the believers and doers of righteous things among them, as well as a magnificent wage.[48]

Another verse (alluded to earlier in this book) lays out a similar description, though this time the sense that this virtue is grounded in God's love is clearer:

> O you who believe! If any among you turns back from their religion, God will bring a people whom He loves and who love Him; they are humble before the believers, but unrelenting before the hostile truth-coverers, striving in God's way, not fearing the blame of any blamer. That is God's grace, which He gives to whomsoever He wills. God is embracing, knowing.[49]

These two verses elaborate a few important points about the traits of ideal believers, when faced with hostility. First, both verses emphasize that they are unyielding, uncompromising, adamant, and one might say "hard" when faced with a certain antagonistic group. That antagonistic group is described as those who are *kāfir*, that is, those who actively seek to erase God's name from remembrance on earth, even by means of violence.[50] Second, the two verses quoted emphasize that these ideal believers are "merciful" and "humble" with those who pose little risk of harm or hostility. In fact, as part of their daily practice, they engage so frequently in acts of humility before God that their foreheads show the marks of frequent prostration. God loves them, and they love Him. That is, these "hard" believers have an even more important "soft" side. These two proclivities tie them to God's own attributes of justice, on the one hand, and mercy, on the other.

This combination of intrepidness and gentleness is a commonplace depiction of the warrior in Islamic ethics. On the one hand, the warrior has no fear of losing his life. On the other hand, the warrior abides by a code of mercy, compassion, and unending love. This becomes clear in an account about Islam's most famous warrior gentleman, ʿAlī ibn Abī Ṭālib, the father of al-Ḥusayn. The account is related by one of Sufism's earliest writers, Abū ʿAbd al-Raḥmān Muḥammad ibn al-Ḥusayn al-Sulamī (d. 1021). ʿAlī ibn Abī Ṭālib appears in al-Sulamī's account because of al-Sulamī's interest in the specific virtue that describes honest and fearless young men, the virtue of youngmanliness (*futuwwa*) mentioned earlier in this book. His example here is telling:

> ʿAlī encountered a handsome young warrior who moved to attack him. His heart filled with pity and compassion for the misguided youth. He cried out, "O young man, do you not know who I am? I am ʿAlī, the invincible. No one can escape my sword. Go and save yourself!" The young man continued towards him, sword in hand. "Why do you wish to attack me?" ʿAlī said, "Why do you wish to die?"

> The young man answered, "I love a girl who vowed she would be mine if I killed you."
>
> "But what if you die?" ʿAlī asked.
>
> "What is better than dying for the one I love?" He replied. "At worst, would I not be relieved of the agonies of love?"
>
> Hearing his response, ʿAlī dropped his sword, took off his helmet, and stretched out his head like a sacrificial lamb.
>
> Confronted by such an action, the love in the young man was transformed into love for ʿAlī and the One whom ʿAlī loves.[51]

For a young man to reach his beloved, ʿAlī is willing to help in the most altruistic way possible, by offering his life. The message here is that love indeed merits laying down one's own life. This action becomes amplified by the identity of the one undertaking it, a figure who "was at the forefront of nearly all the major battles fought under the Prophet's banner" and was "undefeated in all the single-combat duels with which the battles normally began," a figure about whose bravery, service, and *futuwwa* exist numerous statements attributed to the Prophet.[52]

In fact, the Sunni Sufi tradition mirrors the Shiʿi tradition in having a wealth of materials to describe the virtues of the warrior as epitomized by ʿAlī. The celebrated long narrative poem by the Sufi master Jalāl al-Dīn Balkhī, known as "Rūmī," will often paint ʿAlī and his sword as an extension of God's will.[53] In one passage, this becomes incredibly clear, and one sees how the warrior embodies a certain code of pure intentions—even while in combat. Rūmī describes ʿAlī in the middle of battle, on the verge of killing an obstinate enemy of the Prophet and the believers. As he was about to dispatch the enemy to a just death, the man spat in ʿAlī's face. Immediately, ʿAlī threw aside his sword, allowing the man to live. This puzzled the enemy, who seems to have been so moved by this action that he converted to Islam.[54] Still, he sought an explanation from ʿAlī, which appears versified by Rūmī:

> He said: I thrust this blade for the Real.
> I am the Real's servant, not one at the command of the body.
> The Real's lion, I am not the lion of caprice!
> My actions bear witness to my code of piety (*dīn*)
> In battle, I make manifest "You did not throw when you threw,"[55]
> I am like the blade, and the striker is that Sun.
> I've set aside all the furnishings of selfhood:
> Except the Real, I deem it all to be nothing.
> I'm a shadow. The Sun is my lord.
> I'm His doorkeeper—not a veil that hides Him.
> I'm like a blade bedazzled with gems of union—
> In fighting, I don't kill: I bequeath life.
> Blood does not hide the gems of my blade.

When has wind every moved a cloud from its place?
I'm not straw! I'm a mountain of gentleness, forbearance, and justice.
When has a strong gust ever taken away a mountain?[56]

ʿAlī emphasizes that the source of his combative spirit is God's will, which means that his actions must always reflect God's pleasure. (This is the metaphysical orientation of the warrior that I explore in Chapter 3.) Unlike many warriors, motivated by passions such as anger or egoism, this warrior is an extension of the Ultimate Reality, symbolized by the sun. For this reason, he sees himself as restoring life and mercy through battle, and never being an agent of injustice. Because being spit on caused his heart to be filled temporarily by distraction, he knew that, in that moment, he could not perform his duties as he should. So he stopped. He realized, in that instant, that he must always be like a mountain, firm in Godly qualities. When forbearance or gentleness leaves him, he cannot fight. He can only fight when it is done through compassion and love. His ability to reflect on his actions shows stillness in the course of violence, calm in the midst of anger. These qualities render him a noble warrior.[57]

Conclusion

This chapter has served as an exploration of the gentlemanly or "noble" warrior in Islamic ethics, a major theme in Islamic ethical writings. Nobility (or *karam*) is not always associated with battle, but battle seems to serve as its most vivid instantiation. In battle, the balance between God's attributes of mercy and justice becomes a more pressing matter than at other times, and the warrior—as a manifestation of that balance—must be even more cognizant of God's satisfaction in such combative moments. Practices and narratives recounting Karbala often put this balance on display, as an expression of warrior nobility. With this specific application of the warrior ethos in mind, we can now move on to a broader consideration of warriors and the warrior ethos. In Chapter 3, I consider the place of the warrior ethos in the age of modernity—as well as the possibility that it might be lacking or, at least, in need of better myths.

Notes

1 Goldziher (1966, 1:22).
2 Goldziher (1966, 1:24–26).
3 Ibn Ṭalḥa (1997, 254–255). This quotation, which seems to have been quite moving and popular for those writing in the genre of praise for the virtues of the imams, comes from a book on the virtues of Muhammad's family, *Maṭālib al-Saʾūl fī Manāqib Āl al-Rasūl* (*Requests of the Inquisitive One regarding the Virtues of the Messenger's Family*). It is quoted in al-Kāshānī (1960–3, 4:223), as well as al-Irbīlī (2012, 2:463).

4 al-Irbīlī (2012, 2:463–464). This is also quoted in al-Kāshānī (1960-3, 4:223–224).
5 In delineating this, Ibn Ṭalḥa proclaims that bravery is a virtue that cannot be perceived with the eyes and requires instead intuitive insight: Bravery is known by observing its effects in the outside world. See Ibn Ṭalḥa (1997, 251).
6 Ibn Ṭalḥa (1997, 252–253).
7 Ibn Ṭalḥa (1997, 253).
8 Ibn Ṭalḥa (1997, 253).
9 Frolov (1997, 252).
10 Ibn Ṭalḥa (1997, 254).
11 The *Revival* is one of the most widely read treatments concerning virtue in Islamic thought. It consolidates, as one discussion, approaches to virtue found in Islamic treatises on character traits influenced by the Greek tradition, Sufi manuals on moral psychology, and handbooks on normative behavior from the scriptural and legal tradition. Al-Kāshānī's commentary reconciles this book with the Shiʿi tradition and is, in some ways, more of a revision than a commentary.
12 Hyder (2006, 138).
13 Hyder (2006, 140).
14 Hyder (2006, 141).
15 Hyder (2006, 147).
16 Hyder (2006, 147–148).
17 Brickhouse and Smith (1997, 323–324).
18 Cochran (2008, 87).
19 Cochran (2008, 83–84).
20 Langan (1979, 84).
21 Langan (1979, 87).
22 Quran 96:3. This is *al-akram*, the comparative and superlative of *al-karīm*. The name *al-karīm*, an attribute of "your Lord" in Quran 82:6, is mentioned as one of the 99 beautiful names of God in a famous hadith. See, as an example, al-Ghazālī (1995 [1992], 49–51 and 113–114).
23 Quran 44:17.
24 Quran 36:11.
25 Quran 35:3.
26 Quran 49:13.
27 Quran 28:21.
28 Quran 3:57.
29 In al-Ḥusayn's case, of course, citing Moses brings with it a sense of irony, for the "oppressive people" are Muslims who should recognize al-Ḥusayn's nobility, but instead occupy seats of divine authority established by his own grandfather.
30 Quran 28:22; see al-Ṭabarī (2008, 5:230).
31 Moreover, that he reads a correspondence between his narrative and that of Moses shows us that, to him, human affairs follow moral-spiritual patterns, such that any ethical situation has its explanation in the Quran. This particular parallel will be explored in Chapter 3.
32 al-Makkī (2002, 2:47).
33 Quran 58:22.
34 Shirazi (2005, 111).
35 Shirazi (2005, 109).
36 Aghaie (2004).
37 Rahimi (2012, 73).
38 Rahimi (2012, 320).
39 De Sondy (2015, 10); see also Ayubi (2019, 65).
40 Ruffle (2015, 186–188).
41 Szanto (2013, 79–87).

42 Ruffle (2011, 24–25).
43 Ruffle (2011, 28).
44 Cornell (1998, xviii–xix); see also Shaikh (2023, 6).
45 Cornell (1998, 63).
46 Cornell (1998, 64).
47 Both parts of this visitation come from the segment of the visitation treatise focused on greeting the companions of al-Ḥusayn, from "The Visitation of al-Ḥusayn and the Martyrs Recited on the Day of ʿArafa." See Qummī (1997, 577). The final sentence is a reference to Quran 4:73.
48 Quran 48:29.
49 Quran 5:54.
50 Quran 2:217; 22:40; and 61:8.
51 Ali (2020, 10); al-Sulamī (1983, 14).
52 Shah-Kazemi (2006, 15–16).
53 Shah-Kazemi (2006, 175).
54 Rūmī (2018, 1:245, l. 1:3784).
55 The Quranic verse alluded to here emphasizes God's agency in the Prophet's actions on the battlefield, which Rūmī applies to ʿAlī. It is as though God acts when ʿAlī acts: "You (plural) did not kill them, but God killed them. You (singular, referencing the Prophet) did not throw when you threw, but it was God who threw." See Quran 8:17.
56 Rūmī (2018, 1:246, ll. 1:3799–3806).
57 All this was once summarized by a friend of mine and fellow scholar of Sufism, Dr. Zachary Markwith, who observed that "what one finds in ʿAlī is the warrior who wields the sword in battle, while also lovingly maneuvering the pen in the subtleties of calligraphy." ʿAlī is famously the forefather of the art of Arabic calligraphy, as well as the first spiritual master of Sufism after the Prophet. See Schimmel (1984, 3).

3 A Story of War

Revering the Ahistorical Historical Warrior

In the early 1930s, as Hitler and the Nazis were coming to power, two sons of Jewish immigrants living in Cleveland, Ohio, conceived of a supervillain skilled in telepathy. The name of that supervillain playfully used a term that was making its rounds in sci-fi literature: "Superman." Jerry Siegel and Joe Shuster soon revised that character, gave him hair, had him resemble Siegel's father, and made him a redeemer of the weak and a hero to the downtrodden, creating the "Superman" we know today. The word "superman" originated in the philosophy of Nietzsche, whose phrase *Übermensch* had become distorted in popular culture and had come to be associated with Hitler's ideology.[1] Indeed, in later issues of Siegal and Shuster's comics, Superman defended the innocent against antisemites, an ironic turn if, in fact, Superman originated in the minds of his creators as the dark fulfillment of a German nationalist ideology. Even if his creators had not fully appreciated the philosophical implications of their hero, Superman was part of a pattern: Americans created the earliest superhero narratives—including Batman—as a response to the rise of fascism.[2]

In American culture today, superhero narratives have become the most significant source of warrior myths functioning as national narratives. Through them, Americans collectively laugh and weep. They celebrate shared values, such as bravery, self-sacrifice, and loyalty. One might argue, then, that there is little difference between superhero narratives and classical warrior myths that resemble that of al-Ḥusayn's sacrifice at Karbala: Both serve to convey the warrior ethos, and both communicate what is sacred to their audiences. And if, indeed, both function similarly, then other contemporary fictional narratives might take the place of traditional warrior myths.

Let us explore their similarities and differences, because such a comparison helps us appreciate how the narratives upon which we converge shape our moral identities. Karbala captures the sanctity of the Prophet's bloodline, the truth of Islam and the Quran, and the purposefulness of human existence. Superhero narratives capture the sanctity of democratic values, human rights, and American patriotism, which indeed ties American society together much in the same way that religious communities converge upon certain narratives.[3]

DOI: 10.4324/9781003265191-4

As such, superhero films continue a long tradition of such nationalist warrior narratives, even if—in cinema's past—some semblance of historicity or reality was often maintained. *Iron Man* (2008), for example, tells the story of a weapons manufacturer whom a terrorist group called the "Ten Rings" (with clear parallels to the Taliban) capture and plan to execute. While in captivity, under the guise of building a weapon for his captors, he builds a mechanized suit that allows him to escape. He decides to do good for humanity and, in fact, kills the very terrorists who captured him. He maintains a close relationship with the US military, rendered entertaining by a loving sibling antagonism.

In the past, stories of veterans or war heroes—some historical and some not—had a similar cinematic role. Today, however, superhero movies have become the predominant genre of film that Americans will go to the cinema to watch. Most other films have been relegated to streaming platforms. One major exception was a recent film about an aging Navy pilot, *Top Gun: Maverick* (2022). Hollywood analysts took great interest in the fact that a movie unrelated to superheroes could bring audiences back to the theaters, especially older viewers.[4] Nevertheless, in general, superhero films have supplanted the previous model of nationalistic fiction—military stories—as America's warrior narrative of choice.

In much the same way that storytellers in the medieval period excelled at allegory, contemporary storytellers excel at making use of traditional symbols, images, and figures as embellishments, often creating an entertaining pastiche using those traditional elements. This can be observed in many examples, from the virgin birth of the saber-wielding Anakin Skywalker (the Messianic "chosen one" of the *Star Wars* literary world) to Marvel's use of an actual warrior deity from Germanic paganism, namely, Thor. My interest in this chapter is to argue that these two sorts of narrative (traditional warrior narratives and contemporary mass cultural warrior narratives) have differences that should matter to us, that is, as willing participants in either or neither of those narratives. While they differ quite obviously, the difference lies not merely in sanctity or sacredness. Rather, Karbala belongs to a category of warrior myth that has historical claims, first, and metaphysical premises, second. Modern myths tend to lack one or the other of these two and often lack both. The significance of historical myths and metaphysical premises will soon become clear to the reader, but, first, let us consider the shortcomings of modern myths, such as superhero narratives, as a substitute for traditional narratives that encourage the cultivation of virtues grounded in supersensory meaning.

Horkheimer and Adorno on Late Capitalism's Culture Industry

To begin this consideration of failed heroic narratives, I turn to the work of two cultural critics, Theodor W. Adorno (d. 1969) and Max Horkheimer (d. 1973). Their co-authored book, *Dialectic of Enlightenment*, continued the work of their philosophical school of thought, known as the Frankfurt School, which studied the power structures that vitiated Western cultures after World War II. This period of time, called "Late Capitalism," marked a major shift in human activity, especially—for Adorno and Horkheimer—artistic activity.

As mass-manufactured and commercialized pseudo-art began to replace individually crafted and local art, the consumers of that new capitalistic art were undergoing a change as well: People's tastes were becoming as strategically manufactured as the products they consumed. Manufactured narratives came to assume the functions of traditional hero narratives, hence the relevance to our discussion here. In other words, much of this discussion stems from the fact that I share Adorno and Horkheimer's pessimism about modern narratives produced for popular consumption.

There are two very important points that Adorno and Horkheimer make that pertain to this discussion. The first is that modern myths are part of an industry that, at a certain point, did not even feign to present itself as art, that is, as anything meaningful even in just an aesthetic sense. Rather, the declared focus of the film industry on numbers—the revenues of their films and the salaries of their luminaries—sends a message that cinema is "nothing but business," which allows the film industry to "legitimize the trash they intentionally produce."[5] These narratives aim to have wide appeal, to draw in almost everyone, with the result that "no one can escape."[6] There is something ravenous and destructive about popular art as described by these two critics. Sometimes—such as in the case of jazz music—their discussion descends into a European ethnocentrism that does not recognize itself as such.[7] Disliking jazz syncopation as a matter of taste is fine, but building a cultural theory on that distaste is short-sighted and closed-minded. Nevertheless, the authors do provide useful reasoning for their dislikes—and from that reasoning, we can begin to understand how narratives can elevate our human situation or, in the case of manufactured narratives, promote metaphysical illiteracy.

Put simply, contemporary narratives produced by the culture industry exist to make us pleased with a passive state of mind whereby we find contentment in being consumers. While Adorno and Horkheimer would balk at my use of a popular song to illustrate this point, I feel compelled to do so, because of how nicely the lyrics of this song tie their observations to the matter at hand. Perhaps it helps that the song represents a countercultural message. The song "Wish You Were Here" by David Gilmour and Roger Waters of Pink Floyd captures the sense of feeling trapped and mollified by modern life.[8] The song fits Pink Floyd's larger concern with the way in which institutions strip humans of their natural impulse for greatness. Moreover, it uses the image of the warrior as a contrast to pacified, self-concerned, and circumscribed views of the world. Greatness, in the song, is associated with playing a small part in something of significance. The images associated with greatness all carry a sense of victory in the face of struggle and contention: heroes, ashes, hot air, and war. In contrast to greatness stands a life of ease, self-centeredness, and subjection to control—a life that only seems pleasant. In the life of ease, a person enjoys being the center of attention but, in exchange, remains in captivity. Like children, we become pacified by the promise of having our needs met, placing our wants at the front and center of everything.

This brings me to the second of the two points of significance raised by Adorno and Horkheimer. While the authors concerns lie mostly with the social and aesthetic dimensions of late capitalism, they do momentarily turn their gaze upward—toward metaphysics—to state their case. Their view centers on "the culture industry," which refers to the collective of all popular media outlets that create false needs, pacifying consumers and rendering them intellectually impaired. That culture industry presents art, literature, and music in formulaic patterns that appeal to the largest number of people. As such, the culture industry denies a human mental activity that the philosopher Immanuel Kant (d. 1804) theorized, namely, a process whereby the plurality of sensory input that humans receive becomes attached to larger fundamental concepts. According to Kant, the mind has an ability to fit data into paradigms or patterns that suit reason. In place of this, according to the authors, the culture industry provides consumers with classifications, classifications that people enjoy, but also find easy and realistic, so that what is produced makes art and life seem integrated into a whole.[9] This brings about a "withering of imagination and spontaneity."[10]

Adorno and Horkheimer imply that we should concern ourselves with the patterns of perception in our minds, the way in which our ability to categorize what we perceive through our senses changes when we buy into popular contemporary narratives. Traditional global philosophies certainly also encouraged varieties of categorization, ways of perceiving the world, but did so in a manner more cognizant of a human being's place in the universe, as opposed to an isolated perspective focused on individual wants, comforts, and ambitions. The culture industry alters traditional ways of perceiving the world. While, in the past, humans applied imagination to their surroundings to fit what they perceived with the higher principles that they knew, today's humans fall into patterns of seeing the world in the way that producers of culture, such as marketers, wish them to.

Thus, one very significant traditional alternative to the culture industry's paradigms appears in the Quranic framework that comes up so frequently in the Karbala narrative. In this paradigm, human desires—when obeyed—engender a willingness to be passive before tyrants and distracted from the higher callings of the human soul, which lie in knowing the Ultimate Reality, namely, God in the manifestation of His beautiful names.

Karbala as a Way of Seeing the World: Metaphysical Premises

All the major Quranic narratives have resonances of this paradigm: The Quran places awareness of an unseen deity in contradistinction to the ego and passions such as anger, stubbornness, levity, and concupiscence. We have seen al-Ḥusayn himself reference Quranic narratives within the context of his own trials, particularly the Quranic account of Moses and the Exodus, itself a warrior narrative insofar as it describes Moses's vanquishing of a tyrannical power on behalf of his people.[11] This narrative suits al-Ḥusayn's situation because he, like Moses, preached God's obedience to a people gripped by a tyrant's arrogance.

The Quran makes it clear that Pharaoh's people obeyed him—instead of God—because he vitalized their basest instincts. He "deemed them trivial," appealing to their hopes for worldly goods and their fears of worldly deprivation or, in the words of the song mentioned above, convinced them to trade their "hot ashes" for "trees." Having become "a transgressing people," they gave themselves over so fully to those hopes and fears that obeying a tyrant and disobeying God came naturally to them: "He deemed his people trivial, so they obeyed him; they were, indeed, a transgressing people."[12] On the other side was Moses and his brother Aaron. They arrived at the Pharaoh's court as simple shepherds, one of them a fugitive, challenging the entire cultural system that held power over them. Pharaoh had declared, "O courtly assembly, I know of no god for you but me."[13] Yet Moses defied this by proclaiming God to be a superhuman deity, lord over not only the "heavens and the earth" but also Pharaoh himself and his royal forefathers.[14] Moses's was a revolutionary monotheism because it reoriented human thought away from a sociopolitical/human deity to a transcendent/superhuman one.

One has to bear in mind that, in the Quran, the deity toward which Moses redirects Pharaoh's court is much more than a tribal god. Moses's god is, in fact, the Real or the Ultimate Reality. What we know from elsewhere in the Quran is that God is the "light of the heavens and the earth," whose luminescence sheds its light on all things in a series of effusions.[15] God is aware of all things, comprehending them with His life-giving, loving mercy.[16] When humans become distracted from this reality, it is always for something completely unworthy of their attention, because nothing comes close to God, both as a transcendental deity and as an endless source of noble generosity: "O human! What has beguiled you as to your generous (*karīm*) Lord?"[17]

Awareness of this reality changes perception so that the overwhelming truth of God as Ultimate Reality becomes more important than human affairs, including major cases of one's own suffering. Moses risks his life, as well as that of his brother, Aaron, by facing a tyrant, because of this overwhelming truth. This dynamic also applies to al-Ḥusayn, who makes a declaration to that effect at what was arguably the most painful moment on the day of his martyrdom. He had brought his infant son before the enemy during the final hours of his own life. Beseeching them to give water to the child, he instead witnessed them shoot an arrow through his baby's neck. Distraught, al-Ḥusayn threw the child's blood into the sky. He declared, "What befalls me is made easier because it happens before God's eyes, may He be exalted."[18] That is, al-Ḥusayn perceives the affairs of this world—even unspeakably cruel ones—as subject to the will, judgment, and compassion of a divine overseer. In this he finds solace.

Yet again we see why al-Ḥusayn would reference the Mosaic narrative during his trials.[19] The entire Mosaic narrative is framed as an intimacy with the divine that yields acts of bravery with the aim of social justice. Moses meets God as a voice in a burning bush: "Moses, I am God, Lord of all the worlds."[20] That voice informs Moses that He has helped him throughout his life and commands him to commence the mission for which he was destined: confronting Pharaoh.[21] Moses expresses his misgivings but, joined by his brother, undertakes the task. After miraculously bringing his people out of Pharaoh's control, Moses undertakes a spiritual retreat and once again seeks intimacy: "My Lord, show me that I might gaze upon You."[22] Moses's mission begins in intimacy, culminates in a confrontation with the tyrant of his age, and ends in intimacy.

In a similar manner, the narrative of Karbala is one of intimacy with the Ultimate Reality. Al-Ḥusayn's setting out to liberate a city from tyranny; his being cornered in the desert, along with his family and friends; his being deprived of water; his witnessing the murder of those whom he loved most dearly, including his sons and nephews; and, finally, his own martyrdom: These are all—for al-Ḥusayn—facets of his incredibly intimate relationship with God.

We know that al-Ḥusayn's mission began in intimacy, an intimacy that, like Moses's, was maintained throughout even if realized most manifestly in moments of calm. As one example, many around the world recreate one of al-Ḥusayn's exchanges with God, an exchange that occurred well before the events of Karbala. This is a supplication he once recited on a holy occasion, the Day of ʿArafa:

> O God! Make me fear You as if I see You.
> Bring me the joy of being wary of You.
> Do not disgrace me by letting me sin against You.
> Choose the best for me in Your determination,
> and bless me in your apportionment,
> until I do not prefer a hastening in what You have delayed,
> nor do I prefer a delay in what You have hastened.[23]

We also know that, following his confrontation, his mission ended in intimacy. Or, rather, intimacy with God as his true motivation came into focus. Thus, among al-Ḥusayn's last words, as he lay bleeding and thirsty were reported to be, "Resigned in forbearance with Your decree, O Lord! There is no god other than You! O You who aids those who seek aid. I have no lord other than You and no object of worship other than You!"[24] Soon thereafter, with his final moments absorbed in prayer, al-Ḥusayn breathed his last, as his head was severed from his body.

Seeking intimacy with a transcendent being constitutes the metaphysical dimension of Karbala as a way of seeing the world. Through that metaphysical dimension, the narrative's listeners and readers locate themselves in a universe subject to meaningful interpretation. Karbala's Quranic backdrop—as with the metaphysical dimension of many traditional warrior narratives—works as its self-identifying language. The martyred al-Ḥusayn's actions and intentions can only be decoded in a context where he is a servant of God and the grandson of a prophet, both of which become represented by his parallels to Moses, as disclosed by narrators of his life and death. With the metaphysical dimension, the warrior ethos exists for something beyond the aim of most contemporary programs of social ethics that focus on "living together nicely," where "nicely" might mean "in a just way." Rather, a desire to know the Ultimate Reality and transcend transitory life becomes the backdrop for each of the warrior's sacrifices.

For transparency's sake, my positing of a metaphysically oriented warrior ethos draws from an argument that "our relations to and participation in a spiritual order is crucial to having a meaningful life" even if such spiritual order cannot be known or is nontheistic.[25] As such, I reveal the influence of Muhammad Faruque's discussion of selfhood on my own thinking about this virtue:

> This is because if meanings or values are created freely through subjective feelings, they can also be taken back freely, leaving the self in a state of utter desolation. In all, the normative self should neither be too individualistic nor too impersonal; it is also not to be completely detached from the world, busy pursuing its self-enclosed spiritual life on some isolated island. Rather, the normative self explored and proposed in this study is best characterized as anthropocentric and deeply personal, while at the same time transcending individualism through the pursuit of a philosophico-spiritual ideal.[26]

Faruque's carefully crafted argument addresses a variety of conceptions of the self—here and elsewhere mentioning Nietzsche as a prime example of one who argues for a self-constructed version of selfhood.[27] That the warrior ethos across the world has a crucial metaphysical dimension certainly deserves more discussion, debate, and evidence than what I can offer here. That the Karbala presentation of warrior nobility relies on this metaphysical dimension, however, should now be clear.

Nietzsche and the Search for Manliness

In addition to the narrative's metaphysical dimension, a conspicuous historical-heroic motif runs through the Karbala narrative, informing interpretations of Karbala as a virtue-modeling event. That heroic motif takes on expressions that suit local cultures, for the expressions of that heroic motif have had a direct relationship with culturally specific ways of understanding it.[28] One clear case of this is Iraq, one of the major Shiʿi Muslim strongholds in the world. In the nineteenth and twentieth centuries, Shiʿi Islam began to receive initiates from Iraq's nomadic population, expanding the numbers of Shiʿi Muslim Arabs. The Karbala narrative spread among that population, generally in ways that appealed to their values. Thus, two genres of poetry played a part in generating sympathy for the Karbala narrative. The first, called *abūdhiyya*, celebrated the greatness of tribesmen. The second, *hūsa*, was a type of poetry that could be used for grief or for war, in that it created a sense of excitement.[29] In all of this, the virtue most emphasized in capturing the message of Karbala among these tribes was that of "manliness" (*murūʾa* or *muruwwa*). Bravery, honor, chivalry, and the other composite virtues of *murūʾa*: These were the virtues that created a bridge between the tribesmen's understanding of what was virtuous to their appreciation for the plight of al-Ḥusayn and the manliness of al-Ḥusayn's father, ʿAlī.[30]

Such an emphasis on "manliness" is certainly not restricted to traditional societies, nor to those who live outside the city. To what extent, though, does it still have a place in contemporary, Euro-American urban cultures? Certainly, there are fictionalized or semi-fictionalized narratives that might qualify, such as stories of cowboys, nationalist military heroes, athletes, and the manufactured mass media narratives that I mentioned above. These might very well be alternatives to warrior ethos narratives, developments suited to the modern condition. But I have argued that they are not. Rather, they represent a lack—they are placeholders for narratives that once had great cultural significance, but now lurk in the background among other stories. They are not calls to meaningful action, because they lack either metaphysical significance or a sense of historical veracity.

For now, let us consider one particular cultural trajectory, by which the warrior ethos was made into nonbinding stories and then, eventually, rendered—for a lack of a better word—ineffective. That trajectory is the very "Euro-American" one that affects many of us who write and research in universities, whether we study religion, history, or ethics. Described by Nietzsche, this trajectory blossomed in the nineteenth-century Christian-European contexts in which the philosopher lived.

Nietzsche was able to see the ills of his cultural context more clearly than others in his day, perhaps because of contradictions within himself: Physically quite frail and usually sick, he valued manly strength to the point that it drove much of his philosophical thinking. Despite his sickness, Nietzsche was outspoken, and sometimes quite intrepid, when it came to challenging the norms of his time and place. In his most representative writings, he described a European degeneration, a shift from tribal strength to urban complacency. To do so, Nietzsche drew on a binary in Greek myth: the two sons of Zeus, one of whom (Apollo) represented wisdom and self-control, while the other (Dionysus) represented ecstasy and primordial emotion. Nietzsche's interest was in how the ancient Greeks could contemplate death and suffering, while not falling into the despair that Nietzsche saw around him in the Europe of his day. Nietzsche thought that in this model was perhaps an alternative to the pessimism of the German philosopher Arthur Schopenhauer (d. 1860), who offered art and renunciation as distractions from the true terror of existence.[31]

Nietzsche saw Europe's bygone heroism and lost bravery as related to the urbanization process in Europe. European history had favored the weak and the vengeful. Impotent administrator types had shaped the course of European morality, causing to be lost a more traditional heroic warrior virtue. Nietzsche's goal was to reintroduce the warrior ethos to European cultures. As a philologist, he reminded his audience that in ancient Rome, *bonus* signified the "warrior," in the same way that the German *gut* ("good") once signified the "godlike man."[32] These origins had been forgotten, because "good" had ceased to be applicable to the brave warrior-like man. Nietzsche saw the newer modern European emphasis on selfless acts as "good" ones as derived from a "herd instinct."[33]

Of some importance here is that, in his attempts to understand European moral shortcomings, Nietzsche drew on Islam and the name of Muhammad to "provincialize" Christianity, that is, to strip it of the sense of universality that it had acquired for those around him.[34] His interest in Islam, in other words, was that it might provide a relief in which to see European and Christian values. Thus, by living in Tunisia for some time, he had imagined that "my eye and judgement for all things European will be sharpened."[35]

Nietzsche, thus, practiced his own brand of "Orientalism," the study or depiction of "the East," usually Western Asia and North Africa along with areas of Central Asia, and usually from an ethnocentric perspective. As has sometimes been the case with European Orientalists, Nietzsche idealized his object of inquiry.[36] Both like and unlike those Orientalists who saw Islam in a disparaging light, Nietzsche embraced a fantasy that Muslims and Arabs were a warlike people, suspended within an archaic way of life, misogynistic and manly. To Nietzsche, these were redemptive qualities.[37] This brought him to see Islam as a life-affirming religion that offered an opportunity for Europe to undergo a liberative flourishing in medieval Spain, an opportunity that Christianity had "trampled down," much to his lament.[38] Islam was, for Nietzsche, an "affirmative Semitic religion," meaning a religion with Semitic origins that affirmed natural human strengths, especially those of the warrior.[39]

Islam, in other words, resembled early Hebrew religion in being life-affirming. As captured in notebook entries from 1888, Nietzsche had been trying to think beyond the Aryan-Semitic dichotomy that prevailed among Western European intellectual historians. His focus, instead, was on "life-affirming" and "life-denying" outlooks, while still maintaining his condemnatory attitude toward priestly castes. Thus, Nietzsche classified Buddhism, a darling of German intellectuals, as a religion that was both Aryan and life-denying.[40] His views of Islam reduced a variety of religious traditions tied together by the word "Islam" to one imagined, Semitic religion. His placement of Islam in contradistinction to Christian Europe, too, brushed over shared cultural connections and even shared patterns of thought in intellectual history. Nevertheless, the warrior ethos he described, when abstracted from his culturally essentializing claims, did correspond to a phenomenon easily observed in premodern literature preserved and revered by many Muslims.

There might have been traces of nineteenth-century race theory in Nietzsche's narrative of European decline. Nietzsche proclaimed himself that the historical descent into weak-mindedness ran parallel to the rise of the non-Aryan races, those with dark hair and skin and short foreheads, who were once subjects, but conquered the "master race" both in morality and "physiologically," that is, by mixing.[41] Nietzsche associated these racial victors with the priestly life, a life unhealthy in its asceticism and one that ran counter to the vigor of those who might engage in war.[42]

Nietzsche assumed a paradoxical perspective on Jewish influences in his imagined European moral decline. On the one hand, he made antisemitic claims, attributing the malevolence of priests to "Jewish hatred" and a slow triumph over the natural warrior ethos of blond Aryans in Europe.[43] He suggested that the Jewish people, having suffered defeat and succumbed to priestliness, achieved victory through a radical reversal, exalting the suffering, poor, and powerless over their victors.[44] On the other hand, Nietzsche's views of the Hebrew Bible veered from German philosophers preceding him, insofar as he did not sympathize with dismissals of Biblical Israelite narratives.[45] Nietzsche's criticisms centered less on what Arthur Schopenhauer perceived of a worldliness in Judaism and more on the advancement of passivity and renunciation found in the New Testament, but engendered by Jewish rabbinic ("priestly") culture.[46] Consistent with his ethics, Nietzsche contrasted the "Hellenistic" dandy-like values of the New Testament with the Hebrew Bible's "heroic landscape" and a quality he describes as the "naïveté of the strong heart."[47]

The original "instinct" (meaning a moral code so forcefully ingrained since ancient times that it has become natural and assumed) of the Jewish people was to worship tribal gods, especially "their chief war god, whose main job was insurance of victory over enemies."[48] This was the affirmative, Semitic religion that Nietzsche located in Islam. We might call it a "warrior" Judaism. Defeat, however, led to the adoption of a universal god, since a universal or global god meant the promise of a return to victory over all those subject to that one deity. This shift to abstractions leveraged priests over warriors. It culminated in Jesus, a figure detached from politics, who viewed enemies as friends and elevated the base to nobility.[49] Paul, longing for some form of revenge for the political castration of his people, to which Jesus was indifferent, found a way to condemn the victors: Damn them. Thus, political engagement was vacant from Christianity, merely remembered in Judaism, and warrior piety was left by the wayside to be a sign of the uncivilized.[50]

Nietzsche's vision of an engaged Jewish political morality aligned with a revision of Baruch Spinoza (d. 1677). According to Spinoza, Jesus, like Jeremiah, preached submission to oppression, in contrast to Moses's principle of proportionate retribution under a "well-ordered regime."[51] Yet Spinoza, according to Nietzsche, could not endorse the warrior ethic of Judaism fully, because of his awareness that it rejected and opposed all pacifist, apolitical, and submissively interiorized moralities, including the "scientific-philosophic cosmopolitanism" of Europe to which he was attached.[52]

For Nietzsche, "impotence which doesn't retaliate" became—in this new ressentiment moral order—"goodness" itself; "timid baseness" became "humility"; "submission to people one hates" became "obedience"; "cowardice" became "patience"; and a lack of ability for vengeance became known as a lack of desire for vengeance, "forgiveness," the maxim to love thine enemies.[53] Why Nietzsche saw the transformation of value in Europe from the perspective of race theory—the conquest of "Semitic" Christianity over "Aryan" paganism—had much to do with his absorption of the sciences of his day that would have informed his study as a philologist. Nevertheless, his presentation of a Christian dismissal of a warrior code—one that located sin within retaliation and substituted humility for honor—does suit the sources he cited, whether European in origin (such as Aquinas) or valued in Christian Europe (such as Tertullian).[54] Nietzsche's revisionist account, drawing from the founder of eugenics, observes that a certain sort of criminal has arisen from life in a society for which he has been "too strong."[55] In other words, a divergence between nature and society has created a subclass that would have once been warriors, but now falls outside the boundaries of normative behavior.

Overall, Nietzsche's views on religion often seem simplistic and antiquated. As an Orientalist, Nietzsche designates the eastern, Semitic "Other" with characteristics that are un-European. Even if he praises these characteristics, valuing what other Europeans would deplore, neither the subtleties of history nor the careful study of Islam's many cultural manifestations would support most of his conclusions. What interests me, though, is his use of an imagined Islam and—in our case—Islamic myths, to assess and criticize Eurocentric norms. Beyond just Islam, when seen in the context of Buddhist, Taoist, Vedic, Sikh, Zulu, Persian, Hebrew, and Old English historical myths, we might begin to read Nietzsche's evaluation of Islam as a call for historical myths informed by a warrior ethos shared throughout much of the world. In other words, if nothing else, Nietzsche offers a possibility for explaining why the warrior nobility described in the Karbala narrative would require an introduction in European-language studies on moral philosophy.

Why Nietzsche Matters to the Warrior Ethos

What matters here, then, is the narrative that Nietzsche offers, because it captures the aspiration to a virtue lost in the process of becoming civilized in a certain fashion. It conveys an evidenced (even if not watertight) argument that something changed for Europeans. Perhaps if Nietzsche had had greater access to sources on the history of Islam, he would have noticed that a similar trend captured the attention of Muslim historians as well. Famously, the philosophical historian and sociologist ʿAbd al-Raḥman ibn Khaldūn (d. 1382) reflected on changes in Arabian society:

> Bedouins are more disposed to courage than sedentary people. The reason for this is that sedentary people have become used to laziness and ease. They are sunk in well-being and luxury. They have entrusted defense of their property and their lives to the governor and ruler who rules them, and to the militia which has the task of guarding them. They find full assurance of safety in the walls that surround them, and the fortifications that protect them. No noise disturbs them, and no hunting occupies them. They are carefree and trusting, and have ceased to carry weapons.[56]

As opposed to Bedouins (*al-ʿumrān al-badawī*), who—as nomadic people—live in a natural state, those who rely on laws and the enforcement of laws for their safety (*al-ʿumrān al-ḥaḍarī*, or "the sedentary") "grow up in fear and docility and consequently do not rely on their own fortitude."[57]

In his fascinating analysis, Ibn Khaldūn came to a conclusion very similar to Nietzsche: When religious laws become a matter of "learning and craft to be acquired through instruction and education," that is, an academic endeavor similar to the occupation of the priestly caste that Nietzsche rebuked, then "submissiveness to law" becomes a character trait valued by and assumed by civilized people.[58] During the lifetime of Muhammad, however, matters differed, according to Ibn Khaldūn: Divine law came to Muhammad's community as oral "encouragement and discouragement" rather than "a result of technical instruction or scientific education."[59] An inner sense of fortitude, rather than externally enforced laws, drove Islam's earliest social sphere. In other words, Muhammad's community followed their prophet almost as an ethical tribal leader, while they remained free men and women, unconfined by both a state and a clerical apparatus.[60] This hints to us that the trend that Nietzsche discerned in the Europe of his age has probably emerged in any society where law and order take the place of group solidarity, and this certainly is the case for the history of Muslim-ruled societies.

Aside from Europe, as mentioned above, Nietzsche has already given us another example of this shift from free warriors to tamed civilians: The Israelites were—in his own observation—dominated by warriors before they were dominated by a priestly class. In fact, if anything, the marginalization of the warrior ethos occurs broadly, worldwide, and usually goes by the name "becoming civilized." The poet Chaucer captured this shift in his portrayal of a knight and his son, the knight-to-be or "squire," in *The Canterbury Tales*. The knight is brave, noble, warlike, serious, and straight-laced. His son, however, is none of those things. He is a dandy, more interested in his elegant hair, dancing, and entertaining women, than in war.

Rather than try to locate such complex shifts and allocate blame, we might borrow from Nietzsche's analysis tools that help us evaluate the function of both sacred and historical (and sacred-historical) narratives in our societies. This functional approach to history becomes the focus of the French philosopher Paul Ricoeur (d. 2005), in his consideration of Nietzsche's observations concerning history. Through Ricoeur's expansion on Nietzsche, we can begin to reflect on why it matters that warrior myths, such as that of Karbala, are both sacred and historical or, more precisely, both shaped by the ideals of memory and also perceived as historically true.

Embracing the Ahistorical in Historical Myths

My conception of three terms—namely, "historical," "ahistorical," and "historical myth"—draws from a statement made by Nietzsche: "The ahistorical and the historical are equally necessary for the health of an individual, a people, and a culture."[61] Here Nietzsche describes a dichotomy between an animal impulse versus a human one; an impulse to be ever in the present versus an impulse to remember and ruminate; a forgetfulness with no memory whatsoever versus a mental activity so busy and complex that it can cause intellectual paralysis. The first is "ahistorical" and the latter is "historical."[62] History is like the day or like light: It demands cognitive wakefulness as a recognition of concrete circumstances. But the day needs the night; stimulation demands rest; and rest for the ruminators of history is the slumber of forgetfulness, or ahistoricism. Nietzsche describes a sheerly historical perspective, lacking in the ahistorical, as a lethal one, for it creates a degree of "sleeplessness, of rumination, of historical sensibility, that injures and ultimately destroys all living things, whether a human being, a people, or a culture."[63] To think excessively about the past can bring about an intellectual death, when such cogitation is not counterbalanced by the life-giving properties of action, awareness, stillness, and sensory stimulation.

Ricoeur took interest in this question by contemplating Nietzsche's statement. Ricoeur sympathized with Nietzsche's observation about history, one that emphasizes what history *does* more than what history *is*. According to Ricoeur, Nietzsche rightfully rejected the demand that "history be a science," a demand that creates artificial masks of objectivity.[64] The supposedly objective study of history opposes basic human instincts, such as our desire to flourish or our thirst for justice. Instead of addressing human needs, the "academic" approach to history offers a cold and indifferent account of the past. Even today, Nietzsche's description holds true in what one would encounter in most historical studies—including those that attempt to recount the Karbala narrative in self-styled "academic" terms.

Lurking behind such indifference—for Ricoeur—is the "apology of modernity," which describes the creation of normativity regarding the period at hand, the period in which historians live, as a standard which the past can never reach.[65] Living in a seemingly culturally superior present, historians have no real need for the past, other than to report it objectively or, more accurately, render the past an object of study and hence an object of control. This is certainly not "presentism," a term often used to describe a dismissive attitude held toward the past. After all, such historians can often take an excessive interest in an accurately imagined past, an interest that comes close to fetishizing. Rather, histories deprived of the ahistorical participate in a larger "global historical phenomenon" that biases our perceptions. We become attuned to appreciating a constant horizon of new-ness, an onslaught of events, so that what is "modern" is "new," orienting us toward an accelerated sense of expectation for varieties of progress.[66] The past, in this model, exists mainly to serve as points on a line that build to the present and contrast with the present. By participating in this model, while academic histories are both informed and critical, the perspectives that they offer miss what might be called a "human element," namely, a consideration of what the historical moment under scrutiny actually means.

Nietzsche had much to say about this "human element." He took interest in forgetting and remembering as "horizons" of selfhood. In other words, he took interest in "well-being" and "clear conscience," both of which result in "cheerfulness" and "faith in what is to come," such that instinctual predispositions yield psychological outlooks. This brought him to describe the ahistorical and the historical in terms of health, here quoted once again: "The ahistorical and the historical are equally necessary for the health of an individual, a people, and a culture."[67] One's orientation toward history affects how one manages past injustices, whether those perpetuated against oneself or those one has perpetuated against others. More significant here, history facilitates the construction of modes of selfhood.

Such a functional view of history—history as a narrative tool for shaping the identity of a person or people—captures the meaning of "myth" that I have used throughout this book. In this regard, Nietzsche mentioned figures in European history—the philosopher Friedrich Schiller (d. 1805) and his friend, the poet Johann Wolfgang von Goethe (d. 1832)—who found insufficient models in their contemporaries and thus needed to reach into history for liberation from the expressions of shortsightedness around them. Such minds were greater than their own time, thus requiring the greatness of the past for their suffering.[68] Nietzsche compared such a view of history to the ridiculousness of "curious tourists" and "meticulous micrologists" whose climbing of artifacts such as the Egyptian pyramids rightfully annoys those with greater and more honorable ends, particularly those seeking the happiness of a people or all of humanity.[69] The achievements of the past reassure them that their farfetched vision for their nation or for humanity is not impossible.[70] Nietzsche called this "monumental" history.

Opposed to monumental history are those suffering afflictions, who seek in history a statement of justice. Instead of having great aspirations, they—the weak—have a desire to bring others down with them: They seek, in the words of Nietzsche, a history that "judges and condemns," which he labeled "critical history."[71] These categories reflect Nietzsche's particular view of human history as a tension between the strong-willed and the weak-willed, where the weak in Europe won out and steered the reins of culture.

The Warrior Ethos, Dead or Alive?

Karbala's ties to the Prophet, the Quran, and ultimately to God and His wise surveillance of the realm of humans constitutes its metaphysical dimension. As I mentioned, that metaphysical dimension matters because it locates a person in a universe subject to interpretation. Yet Karbala is also historical, and it is here that Nietzsche's analysis has something to offer. History, to many of us, means the pursuit of truths that occurred in the past, devoid of any supernatural or mythic embellishments. That is not what it means here. Echoing Nietzche's call to temper the historical with the ahistorical, I am not very interested in an "accurate" historical account of Karbala, because such accounts—especially when undertaken by historically minded Euroamerican scholars—have often missed the ahistorical and meaningful elements of this narrative.[72] In part, this is because historical narratives do not merely communicate chains of events. Rather, they communicate a set of values and virtues shared culturally by the audience intended by that narrative, even when historians feign otherwise.[73] When a historian—informed by their own values—reads Karbala as an "accurate" chain of events, what lurks behind that reading is the scale of their own values and the dismissal of the values of the narrative's intended audience. One of those values intended within the narrative—which is actually a virtue in Islamic writings—is the nobility of the warrior, as I have discussed. In fact, to me the term "ahistorical" conveys the sense in which myths can be unabashedly *trans*historical. In myth, philosophical truths can outstrip historical facts.

If Nietzsche's warning holds true, then we should study cultural shifts away from narratives that center the warrior ethos, and toward narratives of weakness and enslavement. But where can we see such shifts occur in history, if indeed they have? One possible case of this occurs in Old English literature, where there seems to have remained cultural memories of Christianity's replacing Anglo-Saxon paganism. This is not to say that the warrior ethos disappeared or was replaced. After all, Arthurian legends—which also reflect this transitional period in Britain's past—eventually came to reflect a Christianized warrior ethos. Certainly, moreover, Christianized Britain had no shortage of noble knights in its literary-historical canon. Still, the narratives described here capture a shift away from a certain established warrior ethos, so that we can see how the process might work, particularly how allegory enters as a substitute.

The "Battle of Maldon" references a real battle that took place on 11 August 911 CE, in Essex, England. In the narrative, an English chieftain is being overcome by invading Vikings. The chief—surrounded at all sides—refuses to capitulate. Hope for victory vanishes, as they are greatly outnumbered. The Vikings kill the chieftain, and, at this point, many of his retainers flee. Those celebrated in this Old English poem, however, choose to fight to their deaths, those deaths a testimony to the honor of their chief. They are immortalized in the narrative that recounts their heroism. Interest in this poem has often surrounded the tension within it between the Christian context of its authors and the bleak heroic worldview of its characters. Scholars of English history and literature can look back, beyond Christian teleological narratives that have replaced pagan ones, and use such texts to imagine a pre-Christian warrior ethos.[74]

Contrast this with a later narrative, found in the Old English poem "Dream of the Rood." This poem tells the story of Jesus's crucifixion, yet offers a narrative that seems to be a transitional one in the history of the English insofar as it allegorizes the warrior ethos, placing the warrior ethos in a counterintuitive context. The allegory here presents Jesus as a warrior and the cross as his weapon, which might have served as an apology to those whose warrior code stood at odds with the traditional crucifixion narrative. After all, that narrative—which made sense in its Greco-Roman context—described a grand soul, a great man, allowing himself to be put on a cross and killed without martial resistance. Here, however, Jesus's sacrifice becomes reframed as a battlefield victory over death:

> Then the young hero undressed himself—that was God Almighty,
> strong and courageous-of-mind. He ascended onto the towering cross,
> noble-spirited in the reckonings of many, when he wished to ransom humankind.
> I trembled when the warrior clasped me. Still, I dared not stoop toward the earth,
> or collapse upon the land's surface. No, I had to stand steadfast.
> …
> There they took him harshly, Almighty God,
> bringing him down from that oppressive form of torment.
> The soldiers abandoned me—
> standing there, streaked in blood.
> I was wounded all over with arrows.
> They laid him down, his limbs spent by weariness.
> They stationed themselves by the head of his body,
> beholding him there, Heaven's Prince,
> as he rested there awhile,
> exhausted now because of the great battle.[75]

The "rood" or cross describes Jesus as a battle-worn warrior taking his means of execution, the cross, as one might wield a weapon, or at times as "a loyal retainer in the *comitatus* of Christ."[76] Here the Germanic warrior ethic meets the Mediterranean Passion narrative. The conjunction of the two yields a poem where Jesus's surrender to authorities and execution—what might have seemed to an Anglo-Saxon audience to be an unmanly act of capitulation—becomes imbued with a language of military valor. It is a reconciliation in poetry that represents a much longer process of Christianization for the Anglo-Saxons. It represents a slow shift from a "Battle of Maldon" England to one where warriors felt their way of life to be endangered. Of course, that shift cannot be traced to one event, not even to the introduction of Christianity.

Neither of these narratives has much of a place in English-speaking societies today, as far as I know. Yet, in my reading of Nietzsche's response to shifts in European modes of identity, something began to lack when narratives like that of "The Battle of Maldon" lost their significance or lost their means of expression other than the historical.[77] Nietzsche was concerned and, in many ways, distraught because of this very process that had taken place in Europe, a process by which a once brave, heroic, and warlike people had—through a particular expression of Christianity—subverted the now natural human instincts that should encourage strength. Elements of his lament strike me (as they might strike you) as strange, considering the boons of reverence and learning that came with the spread and dominance of the Christian Church. Only one part of that lament matters, however: The possibility that a virtue that brings out the best in human nature can be lost when warrior narratives are either erased or allegorized into near erasure.

That warrior narratives can flourish alongside reverence, learning, and a monotheistic metaphysics can be seen in the Karbala narrative. Thus, al-Ḥusayn places a copy of the Quran in front of him before commencing battle, indicating that God's word is paramount. The Quran here represents God's ever-watchfulness.[78] With God's watchfulness in mind, in fact, al-Ḥusayn sets out toward the battlefield by praying, "O God, You are my source of confidence in every instance of grief and my hope in every adversity."[79] Indeed, he insists on observing the noon prayer at "its earliest prescribed time," even in the midst of battle, revealing his constant reverence for and undying loyalty to the Ultimate Reality.[80]

Aside from these Islamic or perhaps Abrahamic motifs, Karbala captures the refusal to die an ignoble death common to warrior myths. In this and in much else, the narrative parallels "The Battle of Maldon." Much like the chief at Maldon, al-Ḥusayn had been cornered, in his case by forces sent by the governor of the nearby city of Kufa, representing the Umayyad caliphate in Damascus. Much like that chief's retainers, a loyal band said to number less than a hundred stayed with al-Ḥusayn, despite certain death. Torsten Hylén has argued that the Karbala narrative continues a Quranic language of covenants, the covenants believers make with God, as well as to the prophetic figure, or, in this case, saintly successor to the prophet, who represents God.[81] Such covenants, like those oaths of fealty that Anglo-Saxon warriors had made to the chief at Maldon, bind the moral subject to a network of virtues: bravery, self-sacrifice, manliness, and loyalty. While the narratives of al-Ḥusayn and Maldon are similar, their remembrance could not be more different. Al-Ḥusayn's story becomes remembered in religious gatherings by hundreds of millions worldwide and serves as the impetus for the world's largest Muslim pilgrimage.[82] Yet the Battle of Maldon is known by a fairly limited number of students of Old English literature.

Conclusion: The Free and the Compromised

To conclude, let us consider one final claim made by Nietzsche, namely, that history's remembered narratives should yield empowerment, as opposed to an impotent yearning for vengeance. This matters because to remember virtues does not necessitate encouraging their cultivation. If the warrior ethos only serves as a memory of injustice, then it would become the sort of narrative that Nietzsche associates with priestly people, one that encourages weakness and subverts the virtues of the warrior. After all, it would elevate the weak above the strong in an open-ended and cyclical progression.

The Karbala narrative has certainly been a venerational refuge for the oppressed and the downtrodden. In it, the injustices inflicted upon al-Ḥusayn can reflect the wrongs of their own societies, the pains within their families, or the grievances of their sect. Yet judgment and condemnation are only one part of the remembrance. At the hands of an able sermonizer or poet, the narrative becomes a monument to the best of human abilities: patience in the face of certain death; sacrifice motived by steadfast love; honesty, bravery, and hope at the Muslim nation's darkest hour.

Memory of the Karbala narrative serves to preserve the core ethical code of early Muslim life, namely, Arabian nobility. Recitation of the narrative often aims to invoke grief for the injustices endured by the Prophet's family—but that grief has an ethical context. It is not about the cruelty and slayings inflicted upon certain historical figures as historical figures, but rather as types. Sometimes those types are "the father," "the brother," or "the soldier," but more accurately they carry moral weight: "the loving father," "the loyal brother," and "the selfless soldier." Those qualifiers occur within the context of Arabian nobility or *karam*, which, as I have established, comprises a constellation of virtues that underlay Muslim life in the first generations of Islam. The murder of these types is, thus, the murder of a way of life, a simpler time that would come to be replaced by imperial rule, that is, by the premodern state and paid soldiers who fight for rulers who are absent from the battlefield and for objectives that have almost no relationship to the moral framework of the soldiers. As such, the Karbala narrative represents a last stand for the warrior ethos embodied by Muhammad himself, a time before the permanent disconnect between moral leadership and political leadership.

To appreciate the contrast between the emerging imperial order and the previous charismatically led one, consider that al-Ḥusayn faced an army that has been estimated at 30,000 soldiers.[83] Of that number, roughly 4,000 were native to Kufa, many of whom had once sided with al-Ḥusayn, but now fought against him, either in hopes of the governor Ibn Ziyād's reward or in fear of his retaliation.[84]

Conversely, the historian al-Ṭabarī reports that seventy-two souls lost their lives for al-Ḥusayn, indicating that his army was quite small.[85] Thus, the poet al-Ṭirimmāḥ ibn ʿAdī al-Ṭāʾī stated, after meeting with al-Ḥusayn, that he realized al-Ḥusayn had been "forsaken in terms of men, which is why he asked me to hurry back [to support him]."[86] Having earlier seen the troops gathered outside of Kufa to subdue al-Ḥusayn's forces, however, that same poet noted the army's momentous size: "There were so many people there that my eyes had never seen a larger congregation gathered on a single patch of earth."[87] The narrative, thus, establishes an ironic contrast. On the one hand is a massive army, under the command of Kufa's governor and ultimately loyal to the caliph in Damascus. Despite their size, their motivations seem mixed; their intentions seem worldly; and their commander, the governor, is absent. On the other hand is a very small army. Despite their limitations, their motivations seem unified; their intentions seem noble; and their commander, al-Ḥusayn, stays with them until the end, when he meets his own death on the battlefield.

The narrative memorializes the contrast between these two models of Muslim warrior by highlighting moments of heightened encounter between the two, moments when the contrast between the traditional model and the imperial model is most vivid. In doing so, the narrative encourages the freedom of spirit embodied by al-Ḥusayn's soldiers and supporters, as opposed to those confined by their attachment to worldly rewards or by their fear of those ruling them. One clear example focuses on the ironic contrast between two figures, namely, al-Ḥusayn's loyal brother, ʿAbbās ibn ʿAlī, and an archer infamous for his role in killing al-Ḥusayn's supporters, namely, Ḥarmala ibn Kāhil al-Asadī:

> Sibṭ ibn Jawzī in *Tadhkirat al-khawāṣṣ* has narrated from Qāsim ibn al-Aṣbagh al-Mujāshaʿī that at that time when the heads of the martyrs were being brought into Kufa, in the middle of all that, a man with a handsome face was riding a horse with a head hanging from around the neck of his horse—the head of a beardless young man with a face like a full moon and whose blessed forehead showed the signs of frequent prostrations. When the horse would extend its neck, the head of that young man would rise to the horse's knees. Then, again, it would be dragged along the dirt. I asked about the name of the rider as well as the name of the beheaded. He said, "This is the head of ʿAbbās son of ʿAlī ibn Abī Ṭālib. As for me, they call me Ḥarmala son of Kāhil al-Asadī." No more than a few days passed when I saw him again. His face had grown ugly and had become so dark with gloom that you would think it had been plastered

> with tar. I said, "That day when I saw you, no one had the glowing skin or fresh face that you had. Tell me what's happened that you've become so ugly and unsightly." That accursed one wept and said, since that day when I picked up that head, every night when I sleep, two individuals come and take my upper arms and the two openings of my collar and throw me into a fire where I burn until the morning, so much so that everyone in my tribe hears my screams and cries. It will not leave me alone, not even for one night." This was how things were for him until he met the everlasting torment. What remains of the conditions of Ḥarmala occurs in the discussion of Mukhtār ibn Abī ʿUbayda, in its own place. And God is the guardian of success.[88]

Ḥarmala has kept ʿAbbās's head in hopes of collecting the reward promised by the governor, Ibn Ziyād. Yet an action he hopes will bring him accolades becomes reframed in light of Quranic retribution. The eternal shame of killing a noble man for ignoble purposes instantiates itself early, even before his own death. The last line in the passage refers to al-Mukhtār ibn Abī ʿUbayd ibn Masʿūd al-Thaqafī al-Kūfī (d. 687), who led a famous rebellion in the aftermath of Karbala. He is known for exerting vengeance on al-Ḥusayn's killers and harnessing the anti-Umayyad sentiment that followed the murder of the Prophet's grandson to effect governmental change.[89] This, along with the theme of punishment and torment for one of the enemies of al-Ḥusayn, might lead the reader to interpret this passage as an exemplification of Nietzsche's critical history that "judges and condemns." Yet certain important but subtle signs in this account indicate to us that it marks not a vengeful memory of the vanquished but rather the death of a way of life marked by tribal nobility and martial bravery.

To appreciate the contrast between ʿAbbās and Ḥarmala—as representing varying warrior types—one must appreciate two key moments in the Karbala narrative. The first is ʿAbbās's moment of death. With the women and children of his camp suffering from severe thirst, al-Ḥusayn gives his brother ʿAbbās permission to ride out to the scene of battle. The narrative will usually, at this point, focus on ʿAbbās's selflessness in the face of certain death. Here it helps to use a later account, a famous account by the Sunni Naqshbandi figure, a polymath and renowned preacher during the Timurid age, Kamāl al-Dīn Ḥusayn Wāʿiẓ Kāshifī (d. 1504–5). The title of his rendition of events—*Rawḍat al-Shuhadāʾ* (*The Paradisal Garden of Martyrs*)—has become synonymous with recitals of the Karbala narrative in Persian, which are even today called *rawḍa*[90]:

> Fearing his [ʿAbbās's] spear and his sword, those present fled. Once again, he [ʿAbbās] rode his horse to the water, and, once again, one thousand cavalrymen attacked him. ʿAbbās threw his spear into the water and drew his blade. Charging out of the water on horseback, he attacked. The throng would flee from any direction toward which he turned his face—until he

> seized control of the water's bank from them. He went into the water, placing his waterskin there. He had the impulse to drink water, but, in the end, remembered the thirst of Ḥusayn and the women and children of the Ahl al-Bayt (the Prophet's family). Without even a taste of water, he mounted his horse, placing the waterskin over his shoulder. Both cavalry and infantry blocked his way. He clashed with them in combat. Suddenly and without warning, Nawfal ibn Azraq made his way to ʿAbbās, while ʿAbbās was occupied with fighting someone else. Standing behind ʿAbbās, he struck ʿAbbās with his sword. His right arm was severed from the rest of his body. Here is where ʿAbbās recited a warrior-verse (*rajzī*), one couplet (*bayt*) of which was as follows [in Arabic]:
>
> By God, even if they cut off my right arm
> I will zealously protect my religion (*dīnī*) with perseverance (*ṣābiran*).[91]
>
> Its translation would be as follows:
>
> If the enemy has cut off my right arm
> neither from my religion nor from my manliness has anything been lost.
> I will strike with my blade, without any concern for death,
> for my return without water would be blameworthy,
> if I reach water. And if I do not, then,
> it is fine for me to disappear altogether.
>
> Out of a sense of manliness (*mardānigī*), ʿAbbās pulled the waterskin to his left shoulder. Then they cut off his left arm.[92]

ʿAbbās fights to protect—to provide water and even life to those too weak to defend themselves. In this, he embodies the Quranic injunction, phrased as a rhetorical question:

> What is wrong with you that you do not fight in God's way for those deemed weak among the men, women, and children—those who say, 'Our Lord, lead us out of this city whose people are oppressive and bring us an ally from You and, from You, a helper!'[93]

He is outnumbered, and yet does not fear loss of life and limb. His intention could not be clearer: He declares it himself, announcing that his sole purpose is the service of the weak. The writer, Kāshifī, aptly summarizes the many virtues on display here (bravery, selflessness, and resolve) in one word: manliness (*mardānigī*).

Conversely, the narrative presents us with Ḥarmala's defining moment as well, a moment common to most accounts of the Karbala narrative. Here Kāshifī describes al-Ḥusayn's reaction to noticing that his infant son has almost perished from thirst. As Kāshifī mentions, the son's name was either

ʿAlī or ʿAbdallāh.[94] Notice that al-Ḥusayn appeals to what should be shared values, namely, that children should not suffer when men battle—and yet his enemies cannot comply with their own traditional Arabian values, out of deference to the power of the governor, who is absent from the battle scene:

> "O people! Even if you think I've done wrong, this innocent baby has done nothing wrong. Give him a handful of water, because his mother's breast-milk has gone dry from extreme thirst." Those hard-hearted transgressors replied, "We would never give a drop of water to you or your children without Ibn Ziyād's express approval." Then an unmanly one from the tribe of Asad, whom they called Ḥarmala ibn Kāhil, pulled out an arrow and shot it toward Ḥusayn. That arrow went through ʿAlī Aṣghar's throat, passing through it and piercing the arm of Ḥusayn. Ḥusayn pulled that arrow from the throat of that unrivaled child, born to a sinless man. He used his gown to wipe the blood that came from the baby's throat, not letting any of the blood spill onto the earth. He turned toward the tents and asked for the baby's mother. He said, "Come take this martyred infant, so that they can quench its thirst at the Pool of Kawthar [in Paradise]." Shahrbānū [the infant's mother] let out a cry, and the ladies of the Ahl al-Bayt wailed in lamentation.[95]

The contrast between the two figures—ʿAbbās and Ḥarmala—becomes crystal clear in this gruesome scene. The former represents the warrior ethos at its best, while the latter appears as a murderer, not a warrior. Also clear is the narrative's memorialization of the warrior ethos as a freedom of spirit. Remember that al-Ḥusayn had, according to multiple versions of this narrative, freed those around him the night before this stand. Figures, such as ʿAbbās, had no fealty or obligation to remain by his side, but instead acted freely. That freedom became heightened at the moments of their death, where, in the case of ʿAbbās, he declared an utter lack of fear of death, as well as an utter lack of need for his body, whether limbs of that body or his life entirely.

Contrast that with the actors in the scene of the infant ʿAlī's death. So heavy weighs their duty to an absent governor, that they cannot even offer water to a dying infant without his approval. The absence of that governor matters to the narrative. It means that acts of cruelty become almost inevitable, and those carrying them out become moral automatons. Mercy, leniency, or other peaceful detours of action are no option, because the decree has been made by an absent commander. This leads to damnable actions, such as the slaughter of the Prophet's great-grandson, an infant child, but even that becomes embodied by a lack of agency: While ʿAbbās fights with his arms and even his own teeth, Ḥarmala stands removed from the scene of battle, killing from a distance—distanced both in body and in empathy. As a sharpshooter, he is also an onlooker; he risks little in his actions and cares little about their consequences. He is, as I discuss in Chapter 4, similar to a drone operator.

We thus return to the word free, or *ḥurr* in Arabic, a word that comes up frequently in the narrative. In fact, a commander who defects from the opposing army to join al-Ḥusayn, al-Ḥurr ibn Yazīd al-Riyāḥī (mentioned in this book's introduction), has this word as his name, since "al-Ḥurr" means "the free one." In the narrative, al-Ḥusayn only declares al-Ḥurr as "the free one" after al-Ḥurr frees himself from the forces of Ibn Ziyād and chooses to fight to his death in the defense of al-Ḥusayn and his cause: "You are the free one (*al-ḥurr*) just as your mother named you. And you are the free one both in this life (*al-dunyā*) and in the afterlife (*al-ākhira*)."[96] The narrative supports a warrior ethos premised on freedom, not just as autonomy but also as nobility. In the Arabian tradition, as with the Greek and Roman, freedom and nobility are interchangeable. We had seen this previously, with al-Ḥusayn's admonishment to those who sought to approach and mistreat the women and children of his camp, an action that went against the pre-Islamic Arabian code of conduct:

> Woe unto you! If you have no religion and you do not fear the Day of the Return, then at least—in your worldly affairs—be free men of noble traits. Safeguard my camp and my family from the cruel and dissolute among you.[97]

Thus, we have seen in this chapter's concluding example how accounts of Karbala concerned with the "ahistorical" *meaning* of the event comment on historical shifts, all the while preserving the prioritization of the warrior ethos. Its endangerment, if Nietzsche's analysis of European history has truth to it, is always a probability when warriors who live by that ethos become marginalized.

Of course, even if the narrative centers a traditional warrior ethos, it is still quite possible to make use of the narrative to support vicious actions like those undertaken by al-Ḥusayn's opponents: Narratives are tools, and, as Nietzsche and Ricoeur have argued, they can be used to promote a "critical history" (one that merely condemns) or to inspire heroism. Moreover, proponents of heroism on a national level, especially today, often make use of traditional warrior narratives to encourage actors who are just as compromised as Ḥarmala once was. Hence, the implications of this narrative for contemporary life, especially in the context of violence and war, is the topic of Chapter 4.

Notes

1 Livingstone (2015, 139).
2 Livingstone (2015, 193).
3 Superhero narratives function so powerfully in this discourse that they are even used self-referentially as criticisms, revisions, or meta-commentary on these values, such as in Frank Miller's *The Dark Knight Returns* (1986) or Alan Moore's *Watchmen* (1986–1987).
4 Colbert (2022); Hanna (2022); and Panda (2022).
5 Adorno and Horkheimer (2002 [1987], 95).
6 Adorno and Horkheimer (2002 [1987], 97).
7 Adorno and Horkheimer (2002 [1987], 124).

8 Gilmour and Waters (1975).
9 Adorno and Horkheimer (2002 [1987], 98–100).
10 Adorno and Horkheimer (2002 [1987], 100).
11 For a Quranic reading of the basic outline of the Karbala narrative, see Naqvi (2018).
12 Quran 43:54. An instance of this theme occurs in the Karbala narrative when al-Ḥusayn says to the opposing forces:

> All of you rebel against my command and avoid listening to my words. You have curtailed your gifts [to me] because of what is forbidden. Your bellies are filled with what is forbidden. For this reason, God has put a seal over your hearts. Woe unto you! Will you not listen?! Will you not even hear?!

This indicates that the wealth that the tyrant Yazīd and his governor Ibn Ziyād have spent on them has led to their spiritual blindness and moral corruption. See Najmī (2003 [1381 SH], 170–171.)
13 Quran 28:38.
14 Quran 26:23–28.
15 Quran 24:35.
16 Quran 4:35; 7:156; 40:7.
17 Quran 82:6.
18 al-Muqarram (2012, 280).
19 As mentioned in Chapter 2, al-Ḥusayn references verses Quran 28:21 and 28:22, from the Quranic account of Moses, at two different times in the earliest stages of his mission.
20 Quran 28:33.
21 Quran 20:37–44; 28:31–35.
22 Quran 7:143.
23 Qummī (1997, 361–362).
24 al-Muqarram (2012, 290).
25 Vogler (2019, 88–89). Faruque mentions this perspective and this source in Faruque (2021, 239–240). By "spiritual order," I mean that which cannot be known empirically, borrowing from Faruque's insights.
26 Faruque (2021, 265).
27 Faruque (2021, 229).
28 Nakash (2007, 116–117).
29 Nakash (2007, 117, 122).
30 Nakash (2007, 130).
31 Luyster (2001, 9).
32 Nietzsche (2006, 15).
33 Nietzsche (2006, 12).
34 Almond (2010, 151).
35 Almond (2010, 152).
36 King (1999).
37 Almond (2010, 154–155).
38 Almond (2010, 157).
39 Gericke (2011, 448).
40 Lincoln (1999, 65–66).
41 Nietzsche (2006, 14–15, 19).
42 Nietzsche (2006, 16–17).
43 Nietzsche (2006, 18); see also Moore (2000, 13).
44 Nietzsche (2006, 17).
45 Gericke (2011, 446).
46 Gericke (2011, 446–447).

47 Gericke (2011, 447–448).
48 Neumann (1985, 30).
49 Neumann (1985, 32–33).
50 Neumann (1985, 35).
51 Neumann (1985, 36).
52 Neumann (1985, 37).
53 Nietzsche (2006, 27–28).
54 Nietzsche (2006, 29–30).
55 Moore (2000, 5n3).
56 Ibn Khaldūn (1967, 257). This and the following references to Ibn Khaldūn quote the translation by Franz Rosenthal.
57 Ibn Khaldūn (1967, 259).
58 Ibn Khaldūn (1967, 260).
59 Ibn Khaldūn (1967, 260).
60 Ibn Khaldūn (1967, 261). Syed Farid Alatas has explored the implications of Ibn Khaldūn's thought for the development of Muslim states. Of particular significance here is his discussion of Ibn Khaldūn's theory of "group solidarity," which holds a tribe, clan, or family together and precedes the looser affiliations between citizens of a state. See Alatas (2014, 31–37).
61 Ricoeur (2004, 289); Nietzsche (1995, 90).
62 Nietzsche (1995, 88–89).
63 Nietzsche (1995, 89).
64 Ricoeur (2004, 291); Nietzsche (1995, 109).
65 Ricoeur (2004, 294).
66 Ricoeur (2004, 297).
67 Nietzsche (1995, 89–90).
68 Nietzsche (1995, 96).
69 Nietzsche (1995, 96–97).
70 Nietzsche (1995, 98).
71 Nietzsche (1995, 102).
72 See as examples Shoshan (2004, 247) and Wellhausen (1975, 116).
73 White (1973, 369).
74 Robinson (2002).
75 My translation depends on the edited version of the text, as well as introductory essay and notes, in Mitchell and Robinson (2001, 256–263), here 260, lines 39–43 and 60–65.
76 Holderness (1997, 353).
77 I have added to Nietzsche's observation the importance of a metaphysical dimension. In this case, the Anglo-Saxons took an active interest in what lay beyond their immediately perceptible surroundings, which in their case included a pantheon of gods, the most prominent of which was "Wōden" or "Oden."
78 al-Ṭabarī (2008, 5:286). That he calls for musk to wear before battle points to his nobility. See al-Ṭabarī (2008, 5:285).
79 al-Ṭabarī (2008, 5:286).
80 al-Ṭabarī (2008, 5:296).
81 Hylén (2016).
82 Szanto (2020).
83 al-Muqarram (2012, 201).
84 al-Ṭabarī (2008, 5:276). In the words of the man whom al-Ṭabarī attributes with finishing the life of al-Ḥusayn, namely, Sinān ibn Anas:

> Weigh down my mount with silver and with gold: / I murdered the king, screened [in regality]. / I murdered the best of humanity, best in terms of both mother and father, / and the best of them in lineage among all those who claim lineage.

See al-Ṭabarī (2008, 5:307). The fact that Sinān, from Kufa, undertook his actions for financial reward could not be clearer.

85 al-Ṭabarī (2008, 5:307).

86 al-Ṭabarī (2008, 5:274).

87 al-Ṭabarī (2008, 5:274).

88 Qājār (2007, 2:514–515).

89 This led to his functioning as the ruler of Kufa from 685 to 687. See Haider (2021).

90 Subtelny (2011).

91 Kāshifī quotes the first double-line (*bayt*) in Arabic and follows it with his own rhyming Persian translation, hence the discrepancy. The *bayts* that follow the first—since they are only quoted in Persian—are translations of Kāshifī's Persian translation.

92 Kāshifī (2011, 604).

93 Quran 4:75.

94 As the youngest of his sons sharing the name ʿAlī, he would be ʿAlī the Younger, or "ʿAlī al-Aṣghar" in Arabic and ʿAlī Aṣghar in the author's own Persian.

95 Kāshifī (2011, 604).

96 al-Muqarram (2012, 250).

97 al-Ṭabarī (2008, 5:304).

4 No Sword in Hand

Virtual Soldiers and the Caretakers of Memory

In this book's final chapter, I respond to a lingering question: If the remembered warrior ethos matters, is warfare itself ethically desirable? Unequivocally, I would respond "no." War is among the ugliest of human communal endeavors. From an Islamic perspective, the Quran seems to agree when it describes battle as a necessary but detestable reality.[1] In times when the remembrance of God's name must be preserved, or in times when the defenseless need defenders, fighting becomes a duty.[2] Yet the taking of human life carries a tremendous risk in that to kill another human unjustifiably equates killing all of humanity.[3] This tension between the necessity of defense and the sacredness of life establishes the careful parameters of just war in Islamic ethics. Moreover, most of those who inherit and learn from the warrior ethos are not warriors themselves. As I will discuss at the end of this chapter, the myths and rituals that give continued life to the warrior ethos draw from the intensity of warfare to create an ethical model: Such ethical warfare need not and certainly should not be an endless endeavor.

Even the traditional exalted rank of "martyr" (*shahīd*) in Islamic ethics need not refer to the battlefield. The hadith literature, for Sunni and Shiʿi Muslims alike, mentions enduring rewards in the afterlife for martyrs killed on the battlefield—including the ability to intercede for their loved ones.[4] In this sense, the Quranic term—*shahīd*—can be misunderstood as meaning "one who dies in battle." Yet the word means "witness" and can be applied to anyone who has endured a noble death while maintaining their belief in and obedience to God.[5] In this it resembles the English word "martyr," which also derives from a Greek word (*martus*) meaning a "witness," which, in the New Testament, came to refer to those whose very deaths served as testimonies to their faith.[6] That is, the word *shahīd* should convey the sense that one of many possibilities to serve as a witness to the truth of God's words is a noble death on the battlefield in testimony to God's service.

Unfortunately, contemporary Islamist groups have taken advantage of a circumscribed understanding of the term *shahīd* to encourage young men to engage in battle and even "suicide missions." They do so often without consideration of the larger network of noble virtues traditionally associated with a

DOI: 10.4324/9781003265191-5

good end to life, a larger network of virtues intimately tied to bearing witness to God's beautiful names. They do so despite the fact that in classical Islamic law, Sunni and Shiʿi alike, "suicide" operations veer significantly from the concept of noble battle and cannot be said to be Islamically legal, at least not easily.[7]

Equally at fault for oversimplifying Muslims' relationship with warrior narratives are European-language studies that have often failed to abstract Islamic law and ethics from recent encounters with Islamist groups carrying out acts of terror. This has resulted in excellent responses by Islamic studies scholars, such as Bruce B. Lawrence, John L. Esposito, and Juan Cole.[8] Still, in spite of such efforts, Muslims have become associated with acts of violence in much of the world, such as here in America where—according to a 2016 Pew survey—41 percent of Americans believe that "Islam encourages violence more than other faiths."[9]

What follows will not respond to the stereotype of "Islam and violence," but, rather, will explore how the warrior ethos might be a factor for virtuous conduct (including peace-making) when just warfare is impossible. This discussion does, however, comment on recent salient acts of Muslim terror, insofar as statements made by those Muslims most infamously associated with violence lack the language of virtue we have seen in the Karbala narrative. The hazards of neglecting the warrior ethos will occupy our attention later in this chapter, as we consider drone warfare. The chapter concludes with a consideration of the warrior ethos's relevance for those who are not warriors.

In reference to the lacking of the warrior ethos among many contemporary Islamist movements, I refer to Osama bin Laden's "Letter to America." The letter was released in November 2002, around a year after the events of September 11, 2001, which was also around a year after the subsequent US invasion of Afghanistan in October 2001, and around a month after the US Congress had authorized a joint resolution for US military action in Iraq in October 2002. Much more recently, in November 2023, a full 21 years after it was first published, the letter has been removed from *The Guardian*'s website after it began to go viral. So many young Americans found themselves agreeing with the letter—or parts of it—that *The Guardian* decided that, without the proper journalistic context, the document had become more dangerous than it had been at the peak of America's "War on Terror," finally removing the document from their site on 15 November 2023.[10]

Such interest is concerning because it reflects a way of thinking about justified warfare—a tit-for-tat reprisal devoid of the traditional warrior ethos—that seems to resonate with many, whether Muslim or not, today. On its surface, aside from its antisemitic vitriol, the letter might seem quite "morally" inclined, since its key themes are adherence to divine law, the wrongdoings of America and its people, and the right of Bin Laden and his ilk to seek justice:

> Allah, the Almighty, legislated the permission and the option to take revenge. Thus, if we are attacked, then we have the right to attack back.

> Whoever has destroyed our villages and towns, then we have the right to destroy their villages and towns. Whoever has stolen our wealth, then we have the right to destroy their economy. And whoever has killed our civilians, then we have the right to kill theirs.[11]

Bin Laden assumes the tone of a Muslim leader, speaking on behalf of Muslims in Palestine, Chechnya, Kashmir, and elsewhere. Yet the contrast between the rights-based justification of his actions—as opposed to the virtue-based justifications of al-Ḥusayn's we have seen—cannot be clearer. That the letter would appeal to "social justice warriors" using virtual platforms indicates, to me, a common "slave morality" shared by Bin Laden and those angry about injustices in the world but bereft of the warrior ethos. This holds true even if, as *Vox* has reported, only key portions of the text appealed to Gen Z readers.[12] The letter, after all, combines a thirst for vengeance with an enemy that is abstract—an enemy comprised of an entire nation, or an enemy that one never sees face-to-face. Hence, the compassion and even care that the warrior shows toward his enemies have no place.

Compassion in the Context of Battle

Such compassion and care as a function of the warrior ethos appear vividly in the case of the Emir ʿAbd al-Qādir (d. 1883), the heroic and celebrated adversary to French colonialism in Algeria. The Emir was a Muslim warrior and scholar who retained a profound understanding of the Prophet Muhammad's model of nobility in battle, the model I have referred to as "warrior nobility." Moreover, as someone who lived centuries after the Prophet Muhammad, the Emir serves as a clear example of how remembrance of the warrior ethos can guide soldiers (and those for whom they fight) in times of grave injustice, times that can easily create a thirst for vengeance. The key terms used in Islamic studies scholar Reza Shah-Kazemi's essay on the Emir are "chivalry" and "jihad," both of which reflect observations I have made hitherto about the "warrior ethos," and both of which are informed by what the author calls the "ontological imperative of mercy."[13] The Emir's metaphysical perspective serves as his framework for the good, generating meaning in his conduct, conduct that remains beautiful even in the ugly act of warfare.[14] Shah-Kazemi emphasizes how the mercy of the Muslim warrior radiates from the ontological imperative, in which God's mercy is said to "encompass all things" and "take precedence over" His wrath, as described in a hadith.[15] Human mercy, of course, is meant to be modeled on divine mercy, via the principle that God's beautiful names form the basis of beautiful traits in general. The virtues translate God's beautiful names into human ones.

This ontological imperative for mercy informed the Emir ʿAbd al-Qādir's actions in his noble treatment of the hostile French occupiers in the late 1800s, during their reign of terror in Algeria. That reign of French terror included—according to French accounts such as that of the Count d'Hérisson—a pattern of raping Algerian women and collecting the ears of imprisoned Algerian men, "friends or foes."[16] In the face of such hatred and nationalism, the Emir commanded his resistance fighters to capture French soldiers alive and, once captured, to treat them in accordance with the highest standard of Arab hospitality. He provided the soldiers with a Christian priest, who was also treated kindly. The French themselves recognized the upright character of the Emir, such that the Governor-General of Algeria, General Bugeaud, called him "a kind of prophet."[17]

After the Emir ʿAbd al-Qādir and his forces were defeated and he was exiled to Damascus, he continued to serve as a model for the warrior ethos. Tensions between the Druze and Maronite Christian population of that city led to anti-Christian riots, such that every Christian life was in danger. Emir ʿAbd al-Qādir opposed his own Muslim co-religionists, even when they threatened his life, in order to protect the Christians. He had those loyal to him survey the city to find all the Christians that they could, providing refuge to them. He saved over 15,000 Christian lives by some accounts and held throughout that his actions were motivated entirely by his understanding of Islam's principles of conduct.[18] In fact, he called those Muslims who threatened the Christians "ignorant" in their interpretation of Islam as "hardness, severity, extravagance, and barbarity," taking recourse himself in the beautiful patience and divine aid promised by the Quran.[19]

The warrior must be unflinching in generosity and kindness, even toward their enemy, and even in times of limited resources. In the Karbala narrative, al-Ḥusayn's sense of care and empathy in the midst of conflict emerge clearly in an encounter before the day of battle. The forces opposed to al-Ḥusayn, led by al-Ḥurr, stopped at the same location where al-Ḥusayn's caravan had stopped. Al-Ḥusayn generously provided everyone on the opposing side with water, both for themselves and for their camels and horses. One soldier, named ʿAlī ibn al-Ṭaʿʿān al-Muḥāribī, reported that he was especially thirsty, as was his horse, which al-Ḥusayn noticed. Because of a difference in Arabic dialects, the man did not understand al-Ḥusayn, who wanted to give him water. Therefore, al-Ḥusayn lovingly translated the unintelligible word for him, *al-rāwiya* meaning both "camel" and, in the man's dialect, "waterskin." He used a shared vocabulary and addressed the man as his own family: "O son of my brother! Bring the camel (*al-jamal*) down to a kneeling position." Al-Ḥusayn then handed the man a waterskin, but the man's thirst was so severe, that he could not manage it, so it began to spill. Thereupon, with his own hands, al-Ḥusayn quenched his enemy's thirst, as well as that of his enemy's horse.[20] This narrative appears in al-Ṭabarī's account to highlight al-Ḥusayn's caring, even fatherly, attitude toward those who are in the process of cornering him. These opposing forces would then trap him in Karbala, where he and his friends and family would meet their deaths. More significant is the ironic contrast: While al-Ḥusayn shared water at this crucial point, water of limited supply, the governor Ibn Ziyād would later send a letter commanding a cavalry of 500 men to prevent al-Ḥusayn's camp from drinking the water that flowed freely in the nearby Euphrates.[21]

Warfare without the Warrior Ethos

Before we proceed to consider those who benefit from the warrior ethos and yet never see battle, let us consider the possibility that modern warfare leaves little to no place for the warrior ethos. In other words, the nationalistic, large-scale, and technological nature of contemporary warfare might preclude the possibility of realizing traditional means and methods of humanized encounter. Bereft of the virtues that comprise the warrior ethos, modern warfare thus presents a potential vitiation of human life and an immediate one.

Technology here is no accident to this change in human engagement; it is arguably one of its causes. Such technologies of warfare seem to entail a perspective dismissive of traditional warrior virtues. This becomes quite clear in studies on drone warfare, such as that of Christian Enemark. Enemark also makes use of the phrase "warrior ethos," defined somewhat differently from what we have established here. He defines the "warrior ethos" as "a sense of professional identity and purpose built around virtues and rules," which places opposing combatants on equal footing in terms of their responsibilities for just fighting and their lack of blame for the overarching conflict.[22] One element of reciprocity between opposing combatants is the expectation that both sides undertake risk in combat; both sides face significant, even mortal, loss. Courage is the virtue resulting from this mutual risk. Thus, if one side risks little or even nothing—insofar as that side operates a drone remotely—and hence faces no physical risk, resulting in no need for courage, or at least as the author says no need for "physical courage," would it be the case that a new generation of warriors would lack the warrior ethos altogether?

Enemark argues that warrior virtues—honor, duty, courage, loyalty, and self-sacrifice—would be in danger even without drone warfare, having become more unusual to civilians today, as they are "seldom rewarded in the civilian economy," referring specifically to civilian life in America and other analogous national cultures.[23] Even in war, where one would expect those virtues and where they serve a purpose, they seem to be lacking in some forms of combat that erase or mitigate mutual risk, such as drone warfare or, to a lesser extent, sniping.[24] This altered and disembodied mode of engagement resembles the virtual worlds in which many young men and women now live. Drones, or unmanned aerial vehicle (UAV) systems, have been designed to resemble the interface of PlayStation and other video game consoles.[25] That is, to some extent, the pervasiveness of virtual practices has altered both the way we play and the way we kill. If acclaim is any measure of success, the consequences of this shift have been negative: The lack of personal risk, hence courage, and hence perhaps even virtue, yields a lack of public admiration for the fighter at home.[26] Even among enemies, there exists a perception that, while dangerous, American soldiers fear death greatly. The jackets and helmets American soldiers wore in Somalia, for example, brought them to be perceived as "human tanks."[27]

Such care for one's safety might represent an American "instrumentalist" or utilitarian view of war that contrasts strikingly with the manner in which others—those whom Americans fight—can see war, namely, "metaphysically, placing great meaning on the very act of dying for a cause," as says P.W. Singer.[28] Here the author clarifies that he means Muslim fighters, whose view of the warrior ethos or warrior nobility has parallels to the context of al-Ḥusayn, who indeed do see metaphysical and also ethical significance behind the risks of warfare. It is in such communities that the warrior ethos remains vital and alive.

Certainly, American drone operators make sacrifices and might thereby have some share in virtue. They endure psychological fatigue, trauma, and risks, but Enemark argues that the nature of such risk might resemble that of an executioner, in the sense of guilt, trauma, and perhaps public exposure involved, and less that of a soldier, who risks life and limb.[29] In the end, Enemark concludes that the psychological risks involved in operating drones are "probably not enough to make them warriors," because of the lack of physical risk involved.[30] It might seem to matter little whether American or other soldiers are "warriors" or not. If, after all, the requisite virtues are remnants of an expired way of life, so be it. What does indeed matter—and should matter to all those with concern for human well-being—is the resulting lack of compassion in martial actions, which is studied by Robert Sparrow.

Sparrow considers the ideal character of a warrior through the prism of virtue ethics, describing a "warrior code" comprised of "martial" or "warrior" virtues. One qualifies as a "good warrior" by cultivating the martial virtues.[31] Like Enemark, Sparrow brings into doubt the degree of valor involved when killing becomes a "desk job," stripped of risk and done from a great distance. Even if long distance weapons have existed for some time, such as the spear and the sling, the nature of combat has changed in ways that are both quantitative "and perhaps even qualitative."[32] Sparrow considers the most important martial virtues in this context—courage, loyalty, honor, and mercy—weighing the effects of disembodied, robotic agents of war on each.

Drone warfare requires no "physical" courage, even if it might require "moral" courage. Sparrow finds it difficult to imagine a warrior code that exists without physical courage, that is, the threat of harm to one's own body. Even ascribing some other sort of courage to drone operators does not seem to correspond with what takes place in practice. If we were to imagine the courage of drone operators, it might be akin to that of others who make decisions with life-altering ramifications—such as surgeons. While that would not be courage in the traditional martial sense, nor "physical" courage, it might be courage nonetheless. Yet, as Sparrow indicates, a common challenge in commanding drone operators is that they must be reminded that their targets are indeed human beings. Their superiors must be careful to mitigate their enthusiasm for attacking living targets. This seems to indicate a lack of awareness of the gravity of their actions.[33] Moreover, although it is—practically speaking—a benefit that these operators remain less affected or even unaffected by (1) the fervor of war, (2) the pressure of other soldiers, or (3) the heat of the moment, to act in ways that are illegal or uncalculated, this only reinforces the fact that their job lacks the need for moral courage.[34] The normal temptations of the soldier—to act excessively or mercilessly—do not apply to them, on account of the insouciance of the almost robotic setting in which they operate. The isolated environment of their actions renders drone operation unlike the warrior climates we have known and in which men and women have cultivated courage.

Drone operators would also not cultivate the same sense of loyalty to their fellow soldiers, since they have almost no contact with other fighters. At best, their loyalty would be to institutions.[35] This is an especially pertinent point here: The loyalty that al-Ḥusayn's supporters showed him, as we saw, had its origins in two qualifications. First, men swore allegiance to him because of his blood-ties to the Prophet. The Prophet himself was thought to deserve loyalty because of his divine nomination as God's messenger and his status as a moral example, as mentioned in the Quran.[36] Second, as al-Ḥusayn himself argued, his own status came from the effects of that prophetic heritage, which his supporters saw in his person. By this I mean his noble and virtuous characteristics, virtues that prevented him—as he argued—from acquiescing to the tyrannical caliph. Loyalty to an institution, which might better be called "state allegiance," might stem from a legal-rational duty, or perhaps nationalism. It is not that these are less valid forms of loyalty, but they do fundamentally change the relationship of soldiers to one another or their commander. State allegiance can be found among civil servants and civilians. Hence, there is "nothing distinctively 'martial' about loyalty of this sort," Sparrow argues.[37] State allegiance differs from loyalty to one's troop or to one's commanders, in its erasure of the human element, namely, knowing the characteristics of those who have earned the soldier's loyalty.

Like Enemark, Sparrow sees the limitations in honor that drone operators cultivate to stem from the nature of their combat: There is no physical risk. To kill from such a distance, with no opportunity for the enemy to retaliate, simply does not correspond with human conceptions of honor.[38] Moreover, never meeting one's foe means a greater chance of having no sympathy for them, which would not seem to be conducive to honorable conduct.[39] It would also not be conducive to Sparrow's last martial virtue, namely, mercy. Sparrow explores the idea that a visual encounter with the other—in physical form—is necessary for compassion. To see through a camera means to see the representation, and not the reality, of one's terrified enemy.[40] Human mercy requires human contact—lacking for the drone operator. Nevertheless, since ground warfare will be a reality into the foreseeable future, it might become increasingly difficult to promote the martial virtues, which involve risk, when one group of soldiers is completely protected from risk.[41] All this leads Sparrow to conclude that robotic warfare is a "dangerous experiment," one that risks dehumanizing war, even more dehumanizing than the act of killing others must already be.[42] Drones might be necessary to limit casualties, and perhaps drone operators can cultivate the requisite virtues outside of war, through training.[43] Nevertheless, as war-ready nations move forward with adopting this technology, there should be a concomitant interest in responding to the resulting alterations in human attitudes and traits.

The preceding should not be construed as an argument for or against drone warfare. Nor have I intended in any way to idealize militias, violence, or the maintenance of a standing army, in any way. Rather, it is the ethos itself—one manifested in its most demanding form during times of warfare, but maintained and perfected over decades of peace—that seems to offer at the very least a reconsideration of a general American moral trajectory, with resonances beyond America. In times of peace, the warrior ethos, or Islam's warrior nobility, can be a motivation for avoiding murder: Recall the case of ʿUbaydallāh ibn Ziyād, whose assassination at the hands of al-Ḥusayn's cousin Muslim ibn ʿAqīl was precluded by the latter's warrior moral code. Warrior nobility prevents contemptible acts of violence; it does not encourage them. As a second example, warrior nobility prevented al-Ḥusayn himself from giving his allegiance to the caliph, Yazīd ibn Muʿāwiya. His refusal to do so was, in part, in response to Yazīd's widespread application of state violence.

Certainly, the virtues comprised by the warrior ethos still exist and are celebrated. It is, rather, how we might try to do right, the means by which we live, that seems to alter those virtues—perhaps beyond recognition and repair. As a concluding example, I return to the now common phrase "social justice warrior." It speaks to an idealism, and even a sort of courage. On the other hand, it is often also used disparagingly and ironically. There is a perceived lack of risk in many acts of social justice warfare, especially those undertaken through social media outlets. Tweeting and online posting certainly present risks. In certain scenarios, there might be real physical risk involved as well. Yet "warrior" is almost certainly meant only metaphorically in these contexts. Marching in protest, shutting down businesses, and more physically present forms of justice-seeking, however, require much greater risk. We can say that such actions allow a self-transformation or formation of selfhood much different from virtual means of protest. In other words, the warrior ethos gives us a language to think about technology's place in character formation focused on resistance.

Indeed, not only virtual social justice warriors but most of us engage with war merely as a metaphor. One might say that technological advancements, and especially virtual contexts, mean that life itself is largely metaphorical.

Technology mediates our embodied actions, whether we are moving, communicating, or seeing, and thus alters fundamental elements of human experience: speed, presence, and dimensionality.[44] In that process, effort and risk are mitigated, which is indeed the goal. When applied to moral scenarios premised on effort and risk, such as war, one can say that the formation of character once tied to the act might cease to be.

The Warrior Ethos without Warfare

To be kept alive among a people and affect their moral outlook, the warrior ethos's transformative benefits do not require warfare. Even in a utopia without war, the warrior ethos can remain sustained by myths, rituals, and other cultural practices. After all, those of us traditionally exempt or excluded from warfare have also traditionally commemorated the Karbala narrative. This includes women, the elderly, people with disabilities, people living in peacetime societies, and children, that is, most of humanity. Yet—very much unlike virtual pilots conducting drone warfare—in this case we participate in war's moral elements stripped of its tangible elements: Those who keep the Karbala narrative alive practice compassion, bravery, loyalty, and love through mitigated means, through narrative practices. I would contend that such remembrance is an instantiation of the warrior ethos, even when it takes place outside the boundaries of warfare. Thus, one can practice the warrior ethos without warfare and benefit from it as an unrealized moral ideal or—using Mark Alfano's phrase—as a "factitious virtue."

Mark Alfano has investigated the virtues as fictions that work best as exemplars, however unachievable, exemplars that we might imagine ourselves to have cultivated and that shape our behavior through that fiction. He labels the virtues "factitious" virtues, because no one properly possesses them nor do they ever directly result in human action. He supports this contention with numerous studies that support ethical situationism, namely, the view that situation has a far greater effect on our actions than anything internal. Thus, for example, studies have shown that moods, sounds, and even smells are better predictors of moral behavior than disposition.[45] The virtues are, rather, points of human aspiration that help us be better. In other words, they resemble myths, in much the same way that warrior myths convey a larger sense of how-to-be that need not be realized in actuality, not even by warriors themselves. Put elegantly in Alfano's own words, "Aristotle thought that people became courageous by acting courageously; I contend that they become courageous (or near enough) by being called courageous."[46]

Whether or not one agrees with Alfano, his discussion of factitious virtues allows us to think of the warrior ethos—which I have intentionally kept as broadly defined and as loosely applicable as the sources with which I work—as a descriptive ideal that motivates those who remember it. The warrior ethos is idealized and culturally adaptable, as remembered myths themselves tend to be. Rather than being a descriptor of a disposition, the warrior ethos persists as an imagined goal to which one can constantly aspire. Thus, to put it in terms favored by ethicists, instead of offering one "thick" description of the warrior ethos, I have let the central narrative I associate with that ethos do the work; the thickness here, in terms of context, must be provided by each interpreter of that narrative. Indeed, to this day, communities remembering Karbala as an instantiation of the warrior ethos constantly reinterpret that virtue for themselves.

What do I mean by "thickness"? To know a virtue is often as much a lexical issue as a moral one, in that we might struggle to define what, for example, "bravery" means, especially when it can mean different things to differently informed groups of people. This has its origins in observations made by philosopher Bernard Williams (d. 2003) that to say something meaningful is to say something that "involves a descriptive complex to which a prescription has been attached, expressive of the values of the individual or of the society."[47] In this, Williams touched on advances made in the social sciences, particularly the careful "thick" descriptions of actions and their contexts advocated by anthropologist Clifford Geertz. Once we have proper descriptive understandings, then, among those thick value judgments, we can favor some over others based on the way they function in our social worlds.[48]

The case made for "thick" conceptions of character (defining carefully what it means to be "brave" or "chaste") versus "thin" ones (more general statements about how things ought to be or judging something "good" or "bad") suggests that specificity might help us avoid arbitrary value judgments. If I say a person "ought" to eat moderately, or I say a person is "good" for eating moderately, I effectively say, "I deem it good to eat moderately." On the other hand, if I say that a person is "temperate," I offer something more detailed or thicker.[49] I provide a description that indicates a person indulges in something not too much and not too little. John Doris makes the case that even the idea of "temperate" does not tell us much (here in concordance with Alfano), in that what we perceive as temperance depends more on one's situation than on an inherent character trait. A person might be in the proper position to avoid the temptations of excess and insufficient indulgence. Moreover, as those situations vary, a person might be temperate in some things, and not in others. We might say that a person is temperate-regarding-food, but not temperate-regarding-sex. We might, also, take things further and say that a person is temperate-regarding-sweet-foods, but not other foods.[50] It seems to me that these situational virtues, while supported by scientific evidence, do not give us a conception of human formation that is helpful. The infinite situational or "local" traits that would arise from this would—ultimately—need to be brought back to "globalist" claims that hold the virtue together.[51] Thus, we would say that, if a person is temperate-regarding-sweet-foods, wouldn't it be ideal for them to be temperate in other foods, and indeed other pleasures, as well? That very standard, however discordant it might be from our lived realities, allows us to speak about those realities and aspire to globalist virtues.

This allows us, then, to extend the warrior ethos to all those who aim for such excellence—even as an unachievable ideal—while having in mind the narratives that define the virtue. Put differently, the warrior ethos exists in two ways: first, as realized by figures on the battlefield and embedded within the myth that conveys the warrior ethos, and second, as idealized and actualized in some way by those who remember the warrior myth. In the case of Karbala, both categories would apply to al-Ḥusayn's sister, the "first lady" (*ʿaqīla*) of the Prophet's family at that time, Zaynab bint ʿAlī. While Zaynab did not take up arms, such was dictated by her role as a woman, not by her character. Her actions at Karbala, her caring for the other women and their children, her support of her brother, and her testing her brother's supporters are meant, in the narrative, to convey a valor that resembles her brother's. Moreover, regarding the second category, her actions after Karbala add another layer to the warrior ethos: She becomes renowned for the responses she gives to the oppressors who have killed her brother, sons, and family, speaking at the courts of Kufa and Damascus. Thereby, she creates through her words the factitious version of the warrior ethos that will persist through generations of mourners for al-Ḥusayn. (Notice that this differs from allegorizing the warrior ethos to the point of unrecognizability, as we saw in Chapter 3's Nietzschean critique, since Zaynab's remembrance and the remembrance of generations after her preserve Karbala as a detailed warrior narrative, sustaining at all times its sense of historical specificity.)

After the events at Karbala, Zaynab appears as both warrior and one who remembers, particularly in her public censuring of the tyrants that commanded her brother's death, including the caliph Yazīd. Contemporary mourners around the world commemorate those brave words as "the highest form of jihad," such that recounting them has become a regular part of Karbala ceremonies throughout the world.[52] As discussed in Christopher Paul Clohessy's study on Zaynab, *Half of My Heart*, the bravery required in such actions stems from the fact that the killers of her brother, sons, family, and friends were men of power who could have her imprisoned, tortured, or killed with a simple command.[53] In the case of her rebuttals to Ibn Ziyād, Zaynab's bravery and eloquence can only be compared to those of a brave and skilled warrior. Part of this dialogue was quoted in the Introduction and in Chapter 2. In what continues in that famous exchange, Ibn Ziyād says cruelly to the grieving Zaynab, "God has cured my soul from your tyrant [al-Ḥusayn] and the seditious members of your family."[54]

Zaynab's response illustrates her dual role as verbal warrior and one who remembers warriors: "By my life! You have killed my mature men, defamed my family, cut my young branches to pieces and uprooted my lineage! If this cures you, then you are cured!" Taken aback by Zaynab's boldness and the elegance of her words, Ibn Ziyād says, "By my life! This is bravery! Your father was brave, a poet!" Here, Zaynab teaches Ibn Ziyād that the nature of truthful speech requires a divulging of oneself in an utter sense, which she accomplishes not through bravery but rather a sense of overwhelming grief that makes her indifferent to any consequences: "What has a woman to do with bravery? I am too distracted for bravery, but what I speak is my very soul."[55] By saying this, she intensifies the impact of her speech. To balk at the idea that bravery is an exclusively male virtue misses Zaynab's point entirely. Here, virtues and gender roles are merely a backdrop for the injustice that Zaynab wants to bring her audience to realize. She is, in a sense, too busy with her "jihad of words" (to borrow Abir Hamdar's phrase) to care about the classification of her motivations.[56]

In her role as one who pays homage to Karbala (a role that we can share with her), Zaynab bears witness to the moral reality of that event. She is what contemporary philosopher Yuval Noah Harari would call a "flesh-witness" in her having participated, suffered, and endured in her eye-witnessing.[57] She undertakes, therein, the Quranic-prophetic role of "witness" (*shāhid*) to ultimate reality, her testimony (*shahāda*) conveying the emotional and ethical profundity of the warrior ethos.[58] Repeatedly, her words pronounce what would be either underappreciated or misunderstood. Both as a participant and as a survivor, Zaynab frequently sheds light on the gravity of situations—interpreting them for those present:

> The first lady of the Sons of Hashim became dismayed in a most extreme way, which became even more intense when she and the rest of her family heard her brother handling his sword and mending it, all the while reciting these lines that grievously announced his own death:
>
> O Time! Fie on your friendship!
> How many seekers and companions are murdered
> by you each time the sun rises and sets?
> For Time will accept no substitutes,
> and every living thing walks the path:
> How near at hand is the threat of departure!
> Yet the affair rests entirely with the Exalted.
>
> Accompanying the imam [al-Ḥusayn] at that time, in his tent, was [his son and successor] al-Imām Zayn al-ʿĀbidīn [ʿAlī ibn al-Ḥusayn] and the first lady [Zaynab bint ʿAlī]. As for al-Imām Zayn al-ʿĀbidīn, once he heard these verses, he choked up on account of the significance behind them, so he remained silent. He knew that the calamity had already befallen. As for the first lady, she had become certain that her brother had decided to head out to his death. So she clutched at her tender and tortured heart, sprung toward him, dragging the hem of her clothes on the earth, while her eyes filled with tears. She said to her brother:
>
> "O bereavement! O grief! I wish that death would deprive me of life! O Ḥusayn! O Master! O remnant of the Prophet's family (*ahl al-bayt*)! You've resigned yourself to death and lost hope in life! Today my grandfather, God's messenger, has died. Today my mother, Fāṭima the Resplendent

> (*al-zahrāʾ*), has died, as well as my father, ʿAlī, the One Content with God (*al-murtaḍā*), and my brother al-Ḥasan the Pure (*al-zakī*)! O you who remains of the bygone ones and protector of those who have remained!"[59]

Whether factitious virtue or myth, the warrior ethos only becomes realized through the sort of interpretation that Zaynab provides here. In this instance, she reminds us that the loss of the warrior is the loss of the caretaker. The warrior ethos is centrally a matter of care. This should speak to all of us, then, whether devastated by the cruelties of violence or not. Not everyone will see the effects of war. Yet the dictates of compassion and the interconnectedness of humanity suggest that everyone should care about the effects of war, even more particularly those whose governments represent them in sites of engagement, no matter how far away. Similarly, not everyone—even those who see war's effects directly—will be a warrior. Here too everyone bound together by compassion has a stake in what happens on the battlefield. Zaynab's lamentation in many ways resembles all those who have seen their loved ones killed and maimed in battle. They are a reminder of the consequences of armed conflict and often of tyranny.

Nevertheless, she also points to something unique to Karbala: By murdering al-Ḥusayn, his killers have targeted one of the final remnants of the Prophet's legacy, as embodied by his family. With his departure from this world, al-Ḥusayn takes with him everything he has learned and inherited from his mother, father, brother, and, of course, the origin of Muslim ethics: Muhammad, his grandfather. This is not a single man making his way out to the battlefield for his last stand, but rather the last stand of an entire way of life. The warrior ethos is a significant part of that way of life, so that by leaving the world as a warrior, al-Ḥusayn—like his sister—bears witness to the concerns that have shaped his character, namely, obedience to God, self-sacrifice, honesty, bravery, and most of all nobility. The community of those who remember Karbala, then, commemorate a collection of virtues and thus reinforce the moral framework of the warrior ethos.

Remembering the Warrior Ethos: Conclusion

We have examined the dangers of warfare without the warrior ethos and the transformative potential of this ethos in myths that remember historical warriors. Narratives do not create the warrior ethos. Rather, social, economic, political, and cultural circumstances create and shape these narratives, highlighting what matters to a moral community. The absence of such narratives, then, may indicate deeper deprivations within those circumstances. This might explain why substitutions, like the superheroes of Chapter 3, arise. They are efforts to accept such cultural circumstances through metaphors and symbols—a practice that is not new. As an example mentioned in this book, the Old English poet of the "Dream of the Rood" seems to have attempted to forge a lasting poetic and even metaphysical connection between the warrior ethos and the passion of Christ. Whoever composed it almost definitely wanted to harness the transformative power of the warrior ethos that one finds in the "The Battle of Maldon" in the service of something more Christian and less directly affiliated with battle. When the historical dimension disappears from such narratives, however, along with it disappear its claims to reality.

In fact, the full impact of the warrior ethos for those not engaged in physical combat relies on a compassionate awareness of the very real suffering of others. Zaynab's service as a witness to the full significance of the warrior's sacrifice functions as a clear example of this. As her journey continued, she and her nephew ʿAlī, the son of al-Ḥusayn, repeatedly recounted the events publicly, so that those who today commemorate Karbala trace their storytelling rituals to these two eyewitnesses. In the remembrance of al-Ḥusayn and those who accompanied him in battle, the nobility of the warrior becomes a way of engaging with the world that demands honesty, bravery, steadfastness, loyalty, and nobility. Yet the realization that these are not perfectly achieved nor wholly suited to cultivation is not discouraging. After all, embedded in the Karbala narrative is a message that—perhaps with rare exception—the best of humanity has come and gone, and those left can only aspire to imitation. Such imitation results not only from the remembrance and admiration of human exemplars but also from communal agreement that the warrior ethos represents the peak of moral potential.

Notes

1 Quran 2:216.
2 Quran 22:40 and 4:75.
3 Quran 5:32.
4 Cook (2017, 79–80). Praise for those who die in battle is a major theme in Islam's earliest sources. For example, the believers who defend their people and way of life in battle await "one of two excellent things" to happen to them, either victory for the believers or death on the battlefield, which is itself a sort of victory. See also Quran 9:52; Cook (2017, 77).
5 Cook (2017, 78–79).
6 McGarry (1995, 131).
7 Cook (2017, 94–96).
8 Lawrence (1998), Esposito (2003), Cole (2015a), and Cole (2015b).
9 Lipka (2017).
10 Moench and Shah (2023).
11 Bin Laden (2002).
12 Ohlheiser and Zhoi (2023).
13 Shah-Kazemi (2009, 123).
14 In that regard, a French diplomat (Léon Roches) described catching a glimpse of the Emir as he performed his night prayers, after the Emir cared for the shell-shocked Frenchman. Unaware that the diplomat was watching him, the Emir stood and moved in an ecstatic dialogue with God. The Emir's worship so impressed Roches, that he imagined it to resemble the prayers of the "great saints of Christianity." See Shah-Kazemi (2009, 138).

15 Respectively, Quran 7:156 and Shah-Kazemi (2009, 123).
16 Shah-Kazemi (2009, 131).
17 Shah-Kazemi (2009, 131).
18 Shah-Kazemi (2009, 134).
19 See Quran 12:18; Shah-Kazemi (2009, 136).
20 al-Ṭabarī (2008, 5:270).
21 al-Ṭabarī (2008, 5:278).
22 Enemark (2014, 76).
23 Enemark (2014, 78).
24 Enemark (2014, 82).
25 Enemark (2014, 86).
26 Edemark (2014, 88).
27 Enemark (2014, 89).
28 Singer (2009, 312); Enemark (2014, 90). Of interest is Singer's contention that the lack of dual risk and perceived lack of American physical presence on the battlefield might be a partial impetus for attacks on civilians. See Singer (2009, 312–313).
29 Enemark (2014, 95).
30 Enemark (2014, 96).
31 Sparrow (2013, 84–85).
32 Sparrow (2013, 85–86).
33 Sparrow (2013, 94).
34 Sparrow (2013, 95).
35 Sparrow (2013, 97).
36 Quran 33:21.
37 Sparrow (2013, 97).
38 Sparrow (2013, 99).
39 Sparrow (2013, 99).
40 Sparrow (2013, 101).
41 Sparrow (2013, 104).
42 Sparrow (2013, 105).
43 Sparrow (2013, 104).
44 What once demanded much time now happens instantaneously; what once demanded real presence now needs only virtual presence; and what once demanded multiple dimensions of sensory experience now needs only two.
45 Alfano (2013, 46–49).
46 Alfano (2013, 10).
47 Williams (2011 [1985],144).
48 Williams (2011 [1985], 171).
49 Doris (2002, 116).
50 Doris (2002, 62–66).
51 Globalism is a term that Doris uses to designate the counterpart to situationism, insofar as it places an emphasis on personality traits as the main motivator for behavior, requiring observable consistency of behavior regardless of one's situation, predictable stability over repeated instances of parallel situations, and lastly "evaluative integration" in that traits similar to or related to the target trait can also be observed. See Doris (2002, 22–23).
52 Hamdar 93. Of course, as Edith Szanto has noted, some recent depictions of Zaynab have emphasized her frailty as a woman, in order to inspire militia soldiers to protect her shrine in Damascus, which has been the target of attacks by anti-Shiʿi terrorist organizations in the area. See Szanto (2021, 189), as well as Szanto (2019, 180).
53 Clohessy (2018, 159–220).
54 Clohessy (2018, 181). The translated phrases and sentences here and below are Clohessy's.

55 Clohessy (2018, 181). Of course, as Tahera Qutbuddin states, Zaynab's status as a woman protects her from the retributions that her male relatives face, allowing her to serve as a vocal witness to the Karbala narrative when they cannot. See Qutbuddin (2019, 405). Nevertheless, the narratives convey the sense that, as a woman, she must exhibit even greater bravery to face the cruelty of tyrannical men.

56 Hamdar (2009). The rhetoric of Arabic battle orations or, in the case of Zaynab "post-battle orations," has received detailed treatment in a study by Tahera Qutbuddin. See Qutbuddin (2019, 292–332), here 295, though Qutbuddin discusses elements of Zaynab's effective oratory style throughout the book, especially 390–396.

57 Qutbuddin (2019, 403–405).

58 Quran 22:78; 33:45; 73:15.

59 al-Qurashī (2012, 276–277).

Conclusion

This book has explored an idea, one born from a realization that a collection of traits manifested by the idealized warrior seem to be celebrated in some circles, while changed almost beyond recognition or even forgotten in others. Perhaps this has brought the reader to think about the warrior ethos in a new way and to see how the remembrance of the events at Karbala, well over a millennium ago, does more than comment on history, create group cohesion, allow for spiritual catharsis, or the like. Rather, remembering the Karbala narrative continues to generate interpretive energy for an ethical idea: the idea of the virtuous warrior.

Shifts in the way we live could make the warrior ethos irreparably unrecognizable. For now, the cultural climate in which I live has not forgotten the virtuous warrior, although the way in which that memory lives—through fictionalized, symbolic, and often nationalist narratives—suffers from the shortcomings that I discussed. Such fictionalized narratives, unlike traditional warrior myths, lack historical ties to the communities that tell them and metaphysical ties to the universe beyond them.

What might it look like for the traditional warrior ethos to become unrecognizable? One might consider other instances when we have historically failed to recognize virtue as virtue. Thus, for example, in the case of encountering the indigenous peoples of the Americas, colonizers from Europe suffered from an inability to discern their virtue systems. One might think of it as akin to their lack of ability to see native Americans as possessors of technologies—because those technologies did not correspond to anything they had known as such. So, while the British, French, and Spanish thought of native Americans as primitive, these same indigenous societies had cultivated a variety of crops that make up much of the world's diet today, such as maize, beans, squash, tomatoes, potatoes, chiles, tobacco, cocoa, peanuts, and avocados—which were grown in a manner more sustainable than European farming methods. The weight and allure of Europeans' own narrative of progress, through which they had abandoned tribal life, meant that tribal life in the Americas appeared undeveloped. That narrative also meant that the great cities of the Aztec, Maya, and Inca peoples could be dismissed as primitive, because it failed to

DOI: 10.4324/9781003265191-6

include that which fifteenth- and sixteenth-century Europeans saw as marks of civilization.

What is excluded from moral consideration often appears uncivilized to those excluding it. To continue the above discussion, cultural encounters with Native Americans illustrate this point well. Until the twentieth century, the Navajo people (or the Diné) were a seminomadic indigenous tribe of the southwestern United States, while today those Navajo who live in tribal lands lay claim to the largest native reservation in America. Myths have served an important purpose in preserving and conveying Navajo cultural-religious practices. This includes, for example, narratives about a Monster Slayer figure who spares certain monster enemies, modeling restraint for all those who have the upper hand in warfare.[1] Despite the rich ethical tradition of the Navajo, Washington Matthews, an ethnographer and folklorist writing in 1899, saw in them a "primitive people" whose morality was but a "savage ethics … where authority is lax or ill-defined."[2] Perhaps Matthews struggled to appreciate Navajo ethics because he knew not how to perceive them, so different were the two lifeworlds. Euroamerican ethics, premised on duty and "authority," as Matthews himself notes, had little noticeable analogues in a communitarian and matrilinear society whose sense of honor drew from the cosmos's ability to witness moral actions.[3] Such misunderstandings aside, even Matthews knew to look into Navajo myths for their social code, because he noted in them a propensity to live peacefully among one another, "like a band of brothers."[4] Yet, while appreciative of their tribal cohesion, Matthews failed to appreciate or even perceive the existence of Navajo ethics because he seems not to have seen them as "fully human," to borrow a phrase from Linda Tuhiwai Smith.[5]

One might excuse a historian writing in 1899 for his ethnocentric views. Yet it seems to be part of a larger pattern, such that perhaps any society that has the right amount of power and self-importance will fail to see the value in other ways of thought and life. And, increasingly for many, the warrior ethos seems to be becoming an "other" way of thought and life. Or, perhaps, the European shift away from the warrior ethos happened as far back as Nietzsche claimed. Regardless, philosophers today should be aware of the tendency to exclude those who seem uncivilized from their scope of what counts as philosophy. Bryan W. Van Norden has discussed the ethnocentrism that has plagued and continues to plague Western philosophy, from those who adamantly opposed Thomas Aquinas's (d. 1274) study of Muslim philosophers to Kant's racist view of Chinese, Indian, African, and even Native American biological constitutions as incapable of producing educated philosophers.[6] More disheartening is the book's foreword by Jay L. Garfield, who recounts the resistance he and Van Norden faced in advocating a more global approach to philosophy in the co-authored *New York Times* essay that led to Van Norden's book. Instead of embracing the concept that philosophy cannot be limited to a Eurocentric model, many philosophers accused Van Norden and Garfield of political correctness and made baldly racist claims, including that "Native

Americans have not been literate long enough to produce philosophy."[7] Such naysayers to non-Euroamerican philosophy were not medieval monks in frocks or Enlightenment colonizers in tights, but living, breathing philosophers, currently teaching in our very own colleges and universities.

I have posited that the problem is not a "Western" one at all, but rather more closely related to the very process of urbanization that Ibn Khaldūn noticed in West Asian, Central Asian, North African, and Southwestern European societies. Submission to laws renders city-dwellers complacent, so that they lose what Nietzsche called "natural" qualities—such as courage and freedom of spirit. This would explain why Aristotle, tutor to one of history's most successful world conquerors, would disparage his Greek predecessors who walked around armed with swords. That way of life was, even for Aristotle, in the past. In his more civilized world, to walk around armed with swords was a more specialized role than it had been for his ancestors, a development that he considered to be an advancement. While I am certainly no opponent to structures of living that we might call "civilized," there should be some recognition that changes in the way humans orient themselves toward each other and toward the world will involve sacrifice, in this case, the sacrifice of the place of the warrior or, in Aristotle's context, the ubiquity of the warrior.

I conclude by divulging the truth that I have had two reservations in writing this book. The first is with the word "warrior." The reader will have noticed throughout that the warrior functions as a caretaker, imbued with love for God as well as for those around him. Many commentators on Karbala associate the virtues of al-Ḥusayn and the warriors who fell alongside him with a certain kind of loving masculinity identified as manliness, whether *murū'a* in Arabic or *mardānigī* in the Persian texts quoted. That masculinity is clearly a merciful one, a soft counterpart to the cowardly rule-bound masculinity of al-Ḥusayn's opponents. It is the manliness of the Emir ʿAbd al-Qādir caring for his sick enemies, the very French forces that have raped and mutilated his people, in opposition to the vindictive masculinity that one finds in the Islamist propaganda that held our attention so closely in the early 2000s. As I have offered, al-Ḥusayn's own sister, Zaynab, encapsulates the warrior ethos in her rhetoric. This might beg the question: Why does the "warrior" matter so much to the nobility described? As I have tried to illustrate, it is in the unparalleled cultural impact of warrior myths to effect moral motivations. Narratives surrounding the warrior ethos relay a community in its most precarious time. Stakes are always at their highest, and actors and their actions matter to the audience of that narrative in a superlative way.

The second reservation I have had in writing this book is that so much has been said about the ethics of Karbala in Arabic, Persian, Urdu, Turkish, and every other language that Muslims speak—including English—that its title would seem presumptuous in making a claim to concern a topic that cannot belong to one book. On the one hand, yes, the many ethical discussions surrounding the sacred narrative merit attention, much more than I can offer in this humble endeavor. On the other hand, however, this book is about the "ethics" of Karbala in a rather literal way. Namely, ethics here has meant "character traits," as an extension of the Aristotelian study of character traits from which the English word "ethics" derives. Those traits—represented by the warrior ethos—can certainly receive attention within the context of virtue ethics, as they have here. But to do so, as I have argued, one must also be willing to think of character traits in ways that emphasize their context more than any thick definitions. That is, as I have discussed throughout the book, the narrative context of the collection of traits identified as the "warrior ethos" or "warrior nobility" matters each and every time it comes to be. That context might change depending on who is telling the narrative and where they tell it. Yet certain moral themes remain in common with each telling of this narrative and point to a community of moral elites whose time has passed but whose remembered legacy remains. From this has stemmed my emphasis on the term "myth" to describe an event with verifiable claims to historical reality. Indeed, as I have indicated, it seems quite possible that virtues resemble myths in ways that virtue ethicists might not care to admit.

In its consideration of Karbala as the meeting place of historical veracity and ahistorical meaning, this book suggests a novel and hopefully useful approach to the study of Islam's sacred history. Orientalists of the past, as mentioned briefly, tended to overemphasize Karbala as a historical event that should be studied like other historical political events, including the assumption that motivations must be either selfish or somehow irrational. Today that has changed, and yet very often the material and anthropological studies of Karbala's remembrance—as important as they are—overshadow what many of those who remember Karbala claim to be its most valued dimension, which is the ethical. While material studies of remembering Karbala might paint a picture of a community with idiosyncratic practices, they also leave space for other considerations of Karbala as ethically exemplary in a larger sense or, put differently, as having what its practitioners see as a universal message.

Lastly, the nobility of the warrior in the Karbala narrative has one function to which this book has only alluded, but one of great significance. Having taken place less than fifty years after the Quran's final communications to Muhammad's community, Karbala serves as an ethical artifact for a way of life described in that sacred text. We might assume that books remain preserved when their words remain preserved. Yet if the social context of those words disappears or changes, then the words themselves can become clouded by ambiguity or even distorted by false assumptions. In this book's introduction, I recounted the way in which Muslim-ruled lands changed drastically from the time of the Prophet, such that what had been a confederation of tribes became much larger, more urbanized, and even imperial. As I have mentioned, the two opposing sides at Karbala represented that divide. On one side was the largest army that some had seen at that time, following the orders of an absent governor whose authority came from an even more geographically distant caliph. On the other side was the grandson of Muhammad and a small group that was loyal to him as a person, because of who he was as a person.

In his person, for those ready to die supporting him, al-Ḥusayn embodied the nobility that the Quran enjoined upon its audience and ascribed to its prophetic figures, including Abraham, Moses, and Muhammad. Whatever communal conception of care permeated the Quran's original audience must have included a perspective wherein their leader, Muhammad, resembled those ancient Biblical figures, such as Moses, in his relationship with them. As referenced by al-Ḥusayn in his allusions to the story of Moses, it seems likely that that communal conception of care appeared at Karbala. It appeared, moreover, in a moment of great crisis that—by escalating personal risk—thereby accentuated traits of bravery, loyalty, self-sacrifice, self-worth, and sincerity. The Karbala narrative transmits, then, not only the warrior ethos but also a Quranic conception of nobility that resembles other nonmodern virtues in being endangered by changes in how we live, what we know, and what we value. This should matter to us because, no matter how much humanity might imagine itself to progress in terms of technology, medicine, physics, and the like, ethical learning will always be more elusive. Ethical learning will require us to measure some norms against others and entertain the idea that nonmodern norms might have something worth remembering. As this book has proposed, contemporary audiences worried about toxic masculinities, vindictive brutality, unmanned warfare, and the angst of self-centeredness should take seriously both the warrior ethos and the narratives proclaiming that ethos.

Notes

1 Vecsey (2015, 89).
2 Vecsey (2015, 79).
3 Vecsey (2015, 80).
4 Vecsey (2015, 79).
5 Smith (2021, 28).
6 Van Norden (2017, 18 and 21–23).
7 Van Norden (2017, xiii).

Bibliography

Aghaie, Kamran Scot. 2004. *The Martyrs of Karbala: Shiʿi Symbols and Rituals in Modern Iran.* Seattle and London: University of Washington Press.

Alatas, Syed Farid. 2014. *Applying Ibn Khaldūn: The Recovery of a Lost Tradition in Sociology.* London and New York: Routledge.

Alfano, Mark. 2013. *Character as Moral Fiction.* Cambridge: Cambridge University Press.

Ali, Aun Hasan. 2014 (October). "Some Thoughts on the Remembrance of Karbala," *Muharram in Manhattan.* Accessed at https://muharraminmanhattan.com/2014/10/24/karbalathoughts/ on February 21, 2024.

Ali, Mukhtar H. 2020. "*Futuwwa* as the Noblest Character Traits (*Makārim al-Akhlāq*) in Anṣārī's *Manāzil al-Sāʾirīn* with al-Kāshānī's Commentary," *Journal of Islamic Ethics* 4: pp. 8–24.

Almond, Ian. 2010. *History of German Thought: From Leibniz to Nietzsche.* New York and Oxon: Routledge.

Ansari, Hassan Farhang. 2010a (October). "Āqā-yi Muṣṭafā Malakīān wa Tārīkhnigārī-i ʿĀshūrāʾ," *Bar-rasī-hā-yi Tārīkhī.* Accessed at https://ansari.kateban.com/post/4216 on February 25, 2024.

Ansari, Hassan Farhang. 2010b (December). "Adabīyāt-i Maqtal al-Ḥusayn," *Bar-rasī-hā-yi Tārīkhī.* Accessed at https://ansari.kateban.com/post/1715 on February 25, 2024.

Anscombe, Gertrude Elizabeth Margaret. 2005. "Modern Moral Philosophy," *Philosophy* 53: pp. 1–19; here in *Human Life, Action and Ethics: Essays by G.E.M. Anscombe,* edited by Mary Geach and Luke Gormally. Exeter: Imprint Academic. Pp. 169–194.

Aristotle. 1995. *Politics,* translated by Ernest Barker, Revised with an Introduction and Notes by R. F. Stalley. New York: Oxford University Press.

Assmann, Jan. 1997. *Moses the Egyptian: the Memory of Egypt in Western Monotheism.* Cambridge, MA and London: Harvard University Press.

Ayubi, Zahra. 2019. *Gendered Morality: Classical Islamic Ethics of the Self, Family, and Society.* New York: Columbia University Press.

Barton, Carlin A. 2001. *Roman Honor: The Fire in the Bones.* Berkeley and Los Angeles: University of California Press.

Bin Laden, Osama. 2002 (November 24). "Full Text: Bin Laden's 'Letter to America,'" *The Guardian.* Accessed via archive at https://archive.is/t8G1T on January 31, 2024.

Bint al-Shāṭiʾ, ʿĀʾisha ʿAbd al-Raḥmān. 1985. *al-Sayyida Zaynab: ʿAqīlat Banī Hāshim.* Beirut: Dār al-Kutub al-ʿArabī.

Brickhouse, Thomas C. and Nicholas D. Smith. 1997. "Socrates and the Unity of Virtues," *The Journal of Ethics* 1: pp. 311–324.

al-Bukhārī, Muḥammad ibn Ismāʿīl. 2002. *Ṣaḥīḥ al-Bukhārī*. Damascus: Dār Ibn Kathīr.

Cahen, Claude. 1958. "Mouvements populaires et autonomisme urbain dans l'Asie musulmane du moyen age, i," *Arabica* 5: pp. 225–250.

Clohessy, Christopher Paul. 2018. *Half of my Heart: The Narratives of Zaynab, Daughter of ʿAlī*. Piscataway, NJ: Gorgias Press.

Cochran, Elizabeth Agnew. 2008 (April). "Jesus Christ and the Cardinal Virtues: A Response to Monica Hellwig," *Theology Today* 65: pp. 81–94.

Colbert, Stephen M. 2022 (June 2). "*Top Gun: Maverick*'s Box Office Shows Importance of Non-Marvel Audiences," *Screenrant.com*. Accessed at https://screenrant.com/top-gun-maverick-box-office-older-audiences-marvel/ on July 1, 2023.

Cook, David. 2017. "Developing Martyrology in Islam," in *Martyrdom and Sacrifice in Islam: Theological, Political and Social Contexts*, edited by Meir Hatina and Meir Litvak. London and New York: I.B. Taurus. Pp. 76–96.

Cole, Juan. 2015a (February 24). "How 'Islamic' Is the Islamic State?" *The Nation*. Accessed at www.thenation.com/article/archive/how-islamic-islamic-state/ on January 28, 2024.

Cole, Juan. 2015b (November 14). "Top Ten Ways Islamic Law forbids Terrorism," Informed Comment. Accessed at www.juancole.com/2015/11/ten-ways-islamic-forbids-terrorism.html on January 28, 2024.

Cornell, Vincent J. 1998. *Realm of the Saint: Power and Authority in Moroccan Sufism*. Austin: University of Texas Press.

Crone, Patricia. 2003. "The Pay of Client Soldiers in the Umayyad Period," *Der Islam* 80: pp. 284–300.

Dakake, Maria Massi. 2007. *The Charismatic Community: Shiʿite Identity in Early Islam*. Albany: State University of New York Press.

Delehanty, Ann T. 2001. "Virtue, Vice, and Bakhtin: Can Literature Represent Ethics Better than Philosophy?," *Pacific Coast Philology* 36: pp. 32–47.

De Sondy, Amanullah. 2015 [2013]. *The Crisis of Islamic Masculinities*. London and New York: Bloomsbury.

Digby, Simon. 2001. *Sufis and Soldiers in Aurangzeb's Deccan*. New Delhi: Oxford University Press.

Donner, Fred McGraw. 1981. *The Early Islamic Conquests*. Princeton, NJ: Princeton University Press.

Doris, John M. 2002. *Lack of Character: Personality and Moral Behavior*. Cambridge: Cambridge University Press.

Elias, Norbert. 2000 [1994]. *The Civilizing Process: Sociogenetic and Psychogenetic Investigations*, translated by Edmund Jephcott. Oxford: Blackwell Publishing.

Enemark, Christian. 2014. *Armed Drones and the Ethics of War: Military Virtue in a Post-Heroic Age*. London and New York: Routledge.

Erdinast-Vulcan, Daphna. 2008. "The I That Tells Itself: A Bakhtinian Perspective on Narrative Identity," *Narrative* 16: pp. 1–15.

Esposito, John L. 2003. *Unholy War: Terror in the Name of Islam*. New York: Oxford University Press.

Faruque, Muhammad U. 2021. *Sculpting the Self: Islam, Selfhood, and Human Flourishing*. Ann Arbor: University of Michigan Press.

Föllinger, Sabine. 2009. "Tears and Crying in Archaic Greek Poetry (Especially Homer)," in *Tears in the Graeco-Roman World*, edited by Thorsten Fögen. Berlin and New York: Walter de Gruyter. Pp. 17–36.

Frolov, Dmitrii Vladimirovich. 1997. "The Place of Rajaz in the History of Arabic Verse," *Journal of Arabic Literature*, 28(3): pp. 242–290.

Geertz, Clifford. 1973. "The Impact of the Concept of Culture on the Concept of Man," in *The Interpretation of Cultures*. New York: Basic Books. Pp. 33–54.

Gericke, Jaco. 2011. "The Hebrew Bible in Nietzsche's Philosophy of Religion," *Journal for Semitics* 20: pp. 445–469.

al-Ghazālī, Abū Ḥāmid Muḥammad. 1995 [1992]. *The Ninety-Nine Beautiful Names of God: al-Maqṣad al-asnā fī sharḥ asmā' Allāh al-ḥusnā*, translated by David B. Burrell and Nazih Daher. Cambridge: The Islamic Texts Society.

Gilmour, David and Roger Waters. 1975. "Wish You Were Here" [Recorded by Pink Floyd]. On *Wish You Were Here*. Harvest Records and Columbia Records.

Gleave, Robert. 2017. "The Status of the Battlefield Martyr in Classical Shiʿi Law," in *Martyrdom and Sacrifice in Islam: Theological, Political and Social Contexts*, edited by Meir Hatina and Meir Litvak. London and New York: I.B. Taurus. Pp. 52–75.

Goldziher, Ignaz. 1966. *Muslim Studies* (*Muhammedanische Studien*), edited by S. M. Stern, translated from the German by C. R. Barber and S. M. Stern. Albany: State University of New York Press [Chicago: Aldine Publishing Company; London: George Allen and Unwin Ltd.].

Haider, Najam I. 2021. "al-Mukhtār b. Abī ʿUbayd," *Encyclopaedia of Islam, Three*, edited by Kate Fleet, Gudrun Krämer, Denis Matringe, John Nawas, Devin J. Stewart. Leiden: Brill. Online.

Hamdar, Abir. 2009. "Jihad of Words: Gender and Contemporary Karbala Narratives," *The Yearbook of English Studies* 39: pp. 84–100.

Hanna, Patrick. 2022 (July 18). Flying High With *Top Gun: Maverick*, Movio.co. Accessed at https://movio.co/blog/flying-high-with-top-gun-maverick/ on July 1, 2023.

Hodgson, Marshall G. S. 1974. *The Venture of Islam: Conscience and History in a World Civilization*. Chicago and London: The University of Chicago Press.

Holderness, Graham. 1997. "The Sign of the Cross: Culture and Belief in *The Dream of the Rood*," *Literature & Theology* 11: pp. 347–375.

Horkheimer, Max and Theodor W. Adorno. 2002 [1987]. "The Culture Industry: Enlightenment as Mass Deception," in *Dialectic of Enlightenment: Philosophical Fragments*, edited by Gunzelin Schmid Noerr, translated by Edmund Jephcott. Stanford, CA: Stanford University Press. Pp. 94–136.

Hyder, Syed Akbar. 2006. *Reliving Karbala: Martyrdom in South Asian Memory*. Oxford and New York: Oxford University Press.

Hylén, Torsten. 2016. "*The Hand of God Is Over Their Hands* (Q. 48:10): On the Notion of Covenant in al-Ṭabarī's Account of Karbala," *Journal of Qur'anic Studies* 18: pp. 58–88.

Hylén, Torsten. 2007a. "An Attempt at Structural Analysis of the Karbalā' Drama According to al-Ṭabarī," in *Al-Ṭabarī's History: Interpretation and Challenges*, edited by Håkan Rydving. Uppsala: Uppsala University Press. Pp. 25–55.

Hylén, Torsten. 2007b. *Ḥusayn the Mediator*. (Unpublished doctoral dissertation). Uppsala University, Uppsala, Sweden.

Ibn Khaldūn, ʿAbd al-Raḥmān. 1967 [1958]. *The Muqaddimah: An Introduction to History*, Translated by Franz Rosenthal. Three Volumes. Second Edition. New York: Bollingen Foundation [Princeton, NJ: Princeton University Press].

Ibn Ṭalḥa al-Shāfiʿī, Kamāl al-Dīn. 1997. *Maṭālib al-Saʾūl fī Manāqib Āl al-Rasūl*, edited by al-Sayyid ʿAbd al-ʿAzīz al-Ṭabāṭabāʾī. Beirut: al-Balāgh.

Ibn Ṭāwūs, Sayyid. 1998. *al-Luhūf*, edited with a Persian translation by ʿAlī-riḍā Rijālī Tihrānī. Qum: Nubūgh.

al-Irbīlī, Abū al-Ḥasan ʿAlī ibn ʿĪsā ibn Abī al-Fatḥ. 2012. *Kashf al-Ghumma fī Maʿrifat al-Aʾimma*, edited by ʿAlī Āl Kawthar. Four Volumes. Beirut: Dār al-Taʿāru.

Izutsu, Toshihiko. 2002. *Ethico-Religious Concepts in the Qurʾān*. Montreal and Kingston: McGill-Queen's University Press.

Jaʿfarīyān, Rasūl. 2003 [1382 SH]. *Tārīkh-i Siyāsī-i Islām (1): Sira-yi Rasūl-i Khudā*. Qum: Dalīl-i Mā.

al-Kāshānī, Mullā Muḥsin Fayḍ. 1960–1963. *al-Maḥajjat al-Bayḍāʾ fī Tahdhīb al-Iḥyāʾ*, edited by ʿAlī Akbar al-Ghaffārī. Eight Volumes. Tehran: Daftar-i Intishārāt-i Islāmī.

Kāshifī, Ḥusayn Wāʿiẓ. 2011 [1390 SH]. *Rawḍat al-Shuhadāʾ*, edited by Ḥasan Dhū al-Faqārī, ʿAlī Tasnīmī, and Ṣabā Wāṣifī. Tehran: Muʿīn.

King, Richard. 1999. "Orientalism and the Modern Myth of 'Hinduism,'" *Numen* 46: pp. 146–185.

Langan, John P. 1979. "Augustine on the Unity and the Interconnection of the Virtues," *Harvard Theological Review* 72: pp. 82–83.

Lawrence, Bruce B. 1998. *Shattering the Myth: Islam Beyond Violence*. Princeton, NJ: Princeton University Press.

Lincoln, Bruce. 1999. *Theorizing Myth: Narrative, Ideology, and Scholarship*. Chicago and London: The University of Chicago Press.

Lipka, Michael. 2017 (August 9). "Muslims and Islam: Key Findings in the U.S. and Around the World," *Pew Research Center*. Accessed at www.pewresearch.org/short-reads/2017/08/09/muslims-and-islam-key-findings-in-the-u-s-and-around-the-world/ on November 20, 2023.

Livingstone, David. 2015. *Transhumanism: The History of a Dangerous Idea*. NP: Sabilillah Publications.

Luyster, Robert. 2001. "Nietzsche/Dionysus: Ecstasy, Heroism, and the Monstrous," *Journal of Nietzsche Studies* 21: pp. 1–26.

MacIntyre, Alasdair. 2007. *After Virtue: A Study in Moral Theory*. Third Edition. Notre Dame, IN: University of Notre Dame Press.

Mahallati, Mohammad Jafar Amir. 2016. *Ethics of War and Peace in Iran and Shiʿi Islam*. Toronto, Buffalo, London: University of Toronto Press.

Maḥjūb, Muḥammad Jaʿfar. 1999. "Chivalry and Early Persian Sufism," translated by L. Lewisohn and M. Bayat, in *The Heritage of Sufism: Classical Persian Sufism from Its Origins to Rumi (700–1300)*, Vol. 1, edited by Leonard Lewisohn. Oxford: Oneworld. Pp. 549–581.

al-Makkī Akhṭab Khwārazm, Muwaffaq ibn Aḥmad. 2002 [1381 SH]. *Maqtal al-Husayn li-l-Khwārazmī*, edited by Muḥammad al-Samāwī. Two Volumes. Qum: Anwār al-Hudā.

al-Mawlāʾī, ʿIzzat-Allāh and Muḥammad Jaʿfar al-Ṭabasī. 2005. *Maʿa al-Rakb al-Ḥusaynī min al-Madīna ilā al-Madīna* (Vol. 4): *al-Imām al-Ḥusayn fī Karbalāʾ*. Qum: Markaz al-Dirāsāt al-Islāmiyya.

McDonnell, Myles. 2006. *Roman Manliness: Virtus and the Roman Republic*. New York: Cambridge University Press.

McGarry, Michael. 1995. "Martyrdom: Christian View," in *A Dictionary of the Jewish-Christian Dialogue*, edited by Leon Klenicki and Geoffrey Wigoder. New York and Mahwah: Paulist Press. Pp. 131–132.

Mitchell, Bruce and Fred C. Robinson. 2001. *A Guide to Old English*. Sixth Edition. Oxford: Blackwell Publishers.

Mitchell, Jeff. 2019. *On the Decline of the Genteel Virtues: From Gentility to Technocracy*. Cham, Switzerland: Palgrave MacMillan.

Moench, Mallory and Simmone Shah. 2023 (Nov 16). "Why Osama bin Laden's 'Letter to America' Went Viral on TikTok," *Time Magazine*. Accessed at https://time.com/6336280/osama-bin-laden-letter-to-america-tiktok/ on December 3, 2023.

Moore, Gregory. 2000. "Nietzsche, Degeneration, and the Critique of Christianity," *Journal of Nietzsche Studies* 19: pp. 1–18.

al-Muqarram, ʿAbd al-Ḥusayn. 2012. *Maqtal al-Imām al-Ḥusayn*. Beirut: Dār al-Muttaqīn [Najaf: Muʾassasat al-Marāqid al-Muqaddasa al-ʿĀlamiyya].

Najmī, Muḥammad Ṣādiq. 2003 [1381 SH]. *Sukhanān-i Ḥusayn ibn ʿAlī: az Madīna tā Karbalā*. Qum: Daftar-i Intishārāt-i Islāmī.

Nakash, Yitzhak. 2007. "The Muharram Rituals and the Cult of the Saints among Iraqi Shiites," in *The Other Shiites: From the Mediterranean to Central Asia*, edited by Alessandro Monsutti, Silvia Naef, and Farian Sabahi. Bern: Peter Lang. Pp. 115–136.

Naqvi, Sayyid Ali Naqi. 2018 (June 19). "The Qurʾanic Biography of Imam Husayn: A Translation of Sayyid al-ʿUlama's 'Husayn (ʿa) and the Qurʾan,'" translated by Syed Rizwan Zamir. *al-Sidra* (Ahl al-Bayt Islamic Seminary). Accessed at www.aiseminary.org/al-sidrah/qur%CA%BEanic-biography-imam-%E1%B8%A5usayn-translation-sayyid-al-%CA%BFulama-%E1%B8%A5usayn-%CA%BFa-qur%CA%BEan/ on March 1, 2024.

Neumann, Harry. 1985. "The Case against Apolitical Morality: Nietzsche's Interpretation of the Jewish Instinct," in *Studies in Nietzsche and the Judaeo-Christian Tradition*, edited by James C. O'Flaherty, Timothy F. Sellner, and Robert M. Helm. Chapel Hill and London: The University of North Carolina Press. Pp. 29–46.

Nietzsche, Friedrich. 1995. *Unfashionable Observations*, translated by Richard Gray. Stanford, CA: Stanford University Press.

Nietzsche, Friedrich Wilhelm. 2006. *On the Genealogy of Morality*, translated by Carol Diethe and edited by Keith Ansell-Pearson. Cambridge: Cambridge University Press.

Nussbaum, Martha C. 1988. "Non-Relative Virtues: An Aristotelian Approach," *Midwest Studies in Philosophy* 13: pp. 32–53.

Nussbaum, Martha C. 1995. "Aristotle on Human Nature and the Foundations of Ethics," in *World, Mind, and Ethics: Essays on the Ethical Philosophy of Bernard Williams*, edited by J. E. J. Altham and Ross Harrison. Cambridge: Cambridge University Press. Pp. 86–131.

Ohlander, Erik S. 2008. *Sufism in an Age of Transition:* ʿUmar *al-Suhrawardī and the Rise of the Islamic Mystical Brotherhoods*. Leiden and Boston, MA: Brill.

Ohlheiser, A. W. and Li Zhoi. 2023 (November 17). "The Controversy over TikTok and Osama Bin Laden's 'Letter to America,' Explained," *Vox*. Accessed at www.vox.com/politics/23966248/tiktok-osama-bin-laden-letter-to-america-the-guardian on December 3, 2023.

Panda, Bibhu Prasad. 2022 (June 12). "*Top Gun: Maverick*'s Success Taught Us One Thing – Gen X and Millennials Still Rule the Box Office," Fandomwire.com. Accessed at https://fandomwire.com/top-gun-maverick-box-office-gen-x-millennials/ on July 1, 2023.

Pollard, Rachel. 2011. "Ethics in Practice: A Critical Appreciation of Mikhail Bakhtin's Concept of 'Outsideness' in Relation to Responsibility and the Creation of Meaning in Psychotherapy," *American Journal of Psychotherapy* 65: pp. 1–25.

Qājār, Farhād Mīrzā Muʿtamad al-Dawla. 2007 [1386 SH]. *Qamqām-i Zakhkhār wa Ṣamṣām-i Tabbār dar Aḥwālāt-i Mawlā al-Kawnayn Abī ʿAbd-Allāh al-Ḥusayn*, edited by Maḥmūd Maḥramī Zarandī. Two Volumes. Qum: Kitāb-chī.

Qummī, Shaykh ʿAbbās. 1997. *Mafātīḥ al-Jinān*, edited by al-Sayyid Muḥammad Riḍā al-Nūrī al-Najafī. Beirut: Dār Maktabat al-Rasūl al-Akram.

al-Qurashī, Bāqir Sharīf. 2012. *al-Sayyida Zaynab: Rāʾidat al-Jihād fī al-Islām*, Part 36 in the Encyclopedic Series, *Mawsūʿat sīrat Ahl-al-Bayt*, edited by Mahdī Bāqir al-Qurashī. Second Edition. Najaf: Maktabat al-Imām al-Ḥasan.

Qutbuddin, Tahera. 2019. *Arabic Oration: Art and Function*. Leiden and Boston, MA: Brill.

al-Rāghib al-Iṣfahānī. 2006. *Mufradāt: Alfāẓ al-Qurʾān*, edited by Ṣafwān ʿAdnān Dāwūdī. Qum: Ṭalīʿat al-Nūr.

Rahimi, Babak. 2012. *Theater State and the Formation of Early Modern Public Sphere in Iran: Studies on Safavid Muharram Rituals, 1590–1641 CE*. Leiden and Boston, MA: Brill.

Reid, Megan H. 2011. "ʿĀshūrāʾ (Sunnism)," in *Encyclopaedia of Islam, Three*, edited by Kate Fleet, Gudrun Krämer, Denis Matringe, John Nawas, Everett Rowson. Leiden: Brill. Online.

Ricoeur, Paul. 2004. *Memory, History, Forgetting*, translated by Kathleen Blamey and David Pellauer. Chicago and London: The University of Chicago Press.

Ridgeon, Lloyd. 2010. *Morals and Mysticism in Persian Sufism: A History of Sufi-futuwwat in Iran*. Abingdon, Oxon: Routledge.

Robinson, Chase F. 2003. *Islamic Historiography*. Cambridge: Cambridge University Press.

Robinson, Fred C. 2002. "God, Death, and Loyalty in The Battle of Maldon," in *Old English Literature*, edited by R. M. Liuzza. New Haven, CT and London: Yale University Press. Pp. 425–444.

Ruffle, Karen G. 2011. *Gender, Sainthood, and Everyday Practice in South Asian Shiʿism*. Chapel Hill: The University of North Carolina Press.

Ruffle, Karen G. 2015. "Wounds of Devotion: Re-Conceiving Mātam in Shiʿi Islam," *History of Religions* 55: pp. 172–195.

Rūmī, Jalāl al-Dīn Muḥammad Balkhī. 2018 [1397 SH]. *Mathnawī-i Maʿnawī* (MM), edited by Muḥammad-ʿAlī Muwaḥḥid. Two Volumes. Tehran: Hirmis.

Russell, Daniel. 2009. *Practical Intelligence and the Virtues*. Oxford: Oxford University Press.

Salinger, Gerard. 1950. "Was the Futūwa an Oriental form of Chivalry?" *Proceedings of the American Philosophical Society* 94:5: pp. 481–493.

Schimmel, Annemarie. 1984. *Calligraphy and Islamic Culture*. London: I.B. Tauris.

Shah-Kazemi, Reza. 2006. *Justice and Remembrance: Introducing the Spirituality of Imam ʿAlī*. London and New York: I.B. Taurus.

Shah-Kazemi, Reza. 2009. "From the Spirituality of *Jihād* to the Ideology of Jihadism," in *Islam, Fundamentalism, and the Betrayal of Tradition*, edited by Joseph E. B. Lumbard. Revised and Expanded Edition. Bloomington, IN: World Wisdom. Pp. 119–148.

Shaikh, Saʿdiyya. 2023. "Friendships, Fidelities and Sufi Imaginaries: Theorizing Islamic Feminism," *Religions* 14: pp. 1–15.

Shirazi, Faegheh. 2005. "The Daughters of Karbala: Images of Women in Popular Shiʿi Culture in Iran," in *The Women of Karbala: Ritual Performance and Symbolic Discourses in Modern Shiʿi Islam*, edited by by Kamran Scot Aghaie. Austin: The University of Texas Press. Pp. 93–118.

Shoshan, Boaz. 2004. *Poetics of Islamic Historiography: Deconstructing Ṭabarī's History*. Leiden and Boston, MA: Brill.

Singer, Peter Warren. 2009. *Wired for War: The Robotics Revolution and Conflict in the Twenty-First Century*. New York: Penguin.

Smith, Linda Tuhiwai. 2021. *Decolonizing Methodologies: Research and Indigenous Peoples*. London, New York, Dublin: Zed Books.

Sparrow, Robert. 2013. "War without Virtue?," in *Killing by Remote Control: The Ethics of an Unmanned Military*, edited by Bradley Jay Strawser. New York: Oxford University Press. Pp. 84–105.

Subtelny, Maria E. 2011. "Kāšefi, Kamāl-al-Din Ḥosayn Wāʿeẓ," *Encyclopædia Iranica* XV: pp. 658–661.

al-Sulamī, Muḥammad ibn al-Ḥusayn. 1983. *The Book of Sufi Chivalry*, translated by Tosun Bayrak al-Jerrahi al-Halveti. New York: Inner Traditions International.

al-Suyūṭī al-Shāfiʿī, Jalāl al-Dīn (d. 1505). 1992. *al-Musāraʿa ilā al-muṣāraʿā*, edited by Mashhūr Ḥasan Salmān. Jeddah, Saudi Arabia: Maktabat al-Sawādī.

Szanto, Edith. 2013. "Beyond the Karbala Paradigm: Rethinking Revolution and Redemption in Twelver Shiʿa Mourning Rituals," *Journal of Shiʿa Islamic Studies* 6: pp. 75–91.

Szanto, Edith. 2019. "Economies of Piety at the Syrian Shrine of Sayyida Zaynab," in *Muslim Pilgrimage in the Modern World*, edited by Babak Rahimi and Peyman Eshaghi. Chapel Hill: The University of North Carolina Press. Pp. 172–182.

Szanto, Edith. 2020 (September 9). "The Largest Contemporary Muslim Pilgrimage Isn't the hajj to Mecca, It's the Shiite Pilgrimage to Karbala in Iraq," *The Conversation*. Accessed at https://theconversation.com/the-largest-contemporary-muslim-pilgrimage-isnt-the-hajj-to-mecca-its-the-shiite-pilgrimage-to-karbala-in-iraq-144542 on January 10, 2021.

Szanto, Edith. 2021. "Gender and the Karbala Paradigm: On studying contemporary Shiʿi Women," in *The Routledge Handbook of Islam and Gender*, edited by Justine Howe. London and New York: Routledge. Pp. 180–192.

al-Ṭabarī, Muḥammad ibn Jarīr. 2008. *Tārīkh al-Umam wa al-Mulūk*, edited by Muḥammad Abū al-Faḍl Ibrāhīm. Ten Volumes. Beirut: Dār Iḥyāʾ al-Turāth al-ʿArabī.

Thucydides. 1956 [1919]. *History of the Peloponnesian War*, Books I and II, Volume 1 of *Thucydides in Four Volumes*, translated by Charles Forster Smith, Greek and English Edition. London and Cambridge, MA: William Heinemann Ltd. and Harvard University Press.

Van Norden, Bryan W. 2017. *Taking Back Philosophy: A Multicultural Manifesto*. New York: Columbia University Press.

Vasalou, Sophia. 2019. *Virtues of Greatness in the Arabic Tradition*. Oxford: Oxford University Press.

Vasalou, Sophia. 2022. *Al-Ghazālī and the Idea of Moral Beauty*. Abingdon, Oxon: Routledge.

Vecsey, Christopher. 2015. "Navajo Morals and Myths, Ethics and Ethicists," *The Journal of Religious Ethics* 43: pp. 78–121.

Vogler, Candace. 2019. “The Place of Virtue in a Meaningful Life,” in *Self-Transcendence and Virtue: Perspectives from Philosophy, Psychology, and Theology*, edited by Jennifer A. Frey and Candace Vogler. New York and London: Routledge. Pp. 84–92.

Vryonis, Speros. 1965. “Byzantine Circus Factions and Islamic Futuwwa Organizations,” *Byzantinische Zeitschrift* 58: pp. 46–59.

Wellhausen, Julius. 1974. *The Religio-Political Factions in Early Islam*, edited by R. C. Ostle, translated by R. C. Ostle and S. M. Walzer. Amsterdam and Oxford: North-Holland Publishing Company [New York: American Elsevier Publishing Company].

White, Hayden. 1973. *Metahistory: The Historical Imagination in Nineteenth-Century Europe*. Baltimore, MA and London: The Johns Hopkins University Press.

Williams, Bernard. 2011 [1985]. *Ethics and the Limits of Philosophy*. Abingdon, Oxon: Routledge.

Woodruff, Paul. 1991 (Summer). “Virtue Ethics and the Appeal to Human Nature,” *Social Theory and Practice* 17:2 Pp. 307–335.

Zakeri, Mohsen. 1995. *Sāsānid Soldiers in Early Muslim Society: The Origins of ʿAyyārān and Futuwwa*. Wiesbaden: Harrassowitz Verlag.

Index

Note: Page numbers followed by "n" denote endnotes

Aaron 45
ʿAbbās ibn ʿAlī 21, 25n43, 33–34, 59–62
ʿAbd al-Qādir (Emir) 69–70, 85
Abraham 57, 87
Abū Mikhnaf Lūṭ ibn Yaḥyā 12
abūdhiyya 48
Adam and Eve 30
Adorno, Theodor W. 42–44
Aghaie, Kamran Scot 32–33
ʿĀʾisha bint Abī Bakr 18
Alfano, Mark 75–76
ʿAlī al-Aṣghar 45, 61–62
ʿAlī ibn Abī Tālib 7, 22, 28–29, 32, 36–38, 48, 79
Anscombe, G.E.M. 13
Apollo 48
Aquinas, Thomas 29, 51, 84
ʿArafa, Day of 46
Aristotle 13–17, 29, 75, 85
Aryanism 49–51
ʿĀshūrā, Day of 2, 19
Augustine 29–30
ʿayyārān 4

Batman 41
Bentham, Jeremy 13
Bin Laden, Osama 68–69
bravery: ʿAbbās's 21; ʿAlī's 37; Arab 20, 24; complexities of 12; al-Ḥusayn's 27–28, 79–80; in Karbala narrative 60–61, 75–76, 87; and manliness 48; Moses's 46; Nietzsche 49; Zaynab's 32, 77–78
Buddha, the (Siddhārtha Gautama) 12
Bugeaud, Thomas Robert (General) 70

Cervantes, Miguel de 4
Chaucer 52
chivalry 26, 48, 69; see also *futuwwa*; *murūʾa*
Christ *see* Jesus
Christianity 3, 12–13, 29, 49–51, 57
Clohessy, Christopher Paul 77
Cole, Juan 68
Cornell, Vincent 34

D'Hérisson, Irisson (Count) 70
Dionysus 48
dīwān 18
Don Quixote 4
Doris, John 76

Enemark, Christian 71–73
Esposito, John L. 68

Fārābī, Abū Naṣr al- 4
Faruque, Muhammad 47
Fāṭima bint Muḥammad 7, 25n43, 28–29, 32, 34–35, 78
fityān 4
Foot, Philippa 13
Foucault, Michel 34
free men 5, 20, 52, 58–63
futuwwa 5, 26, 36–37

Garfield, Jay L. 84
Geertz, Clifford 15, 76
Ghazālī, Abū Ḥāmid al- 28
Goethe, Johann Wolfgang von 54
Goldziher, Ignaz 26

Hajj 18
Hamdar, Abir 78
Ḥanafī, Saʿd ibn ʿAbdallāh al- 20
Hāniʾ ibn ʿUrwa 23
Harari, Yuval Noah 78
Ḥarmala ibn Kāhil 59–63
heroism 1–3, 5, 7, 9, 29, 32, 49, 56, 63, 79
Hitler, Adolph 41
Homer 2
honestum 24
honor 20–21, 26, 30–31, 48, 51, 56, 71–73, 84
Horkheimer, Max 42–44
ḥurr (*aḥrār*) *see* free men
Ḥurr ibn Yazīd, al- 6–7, 63, 70
hūsa 48
Ḥusayn, al-: commemeration of 1, 11–12, 19, 32–34, 80; compared to Moses 45–46; followers of 19, 21, 59–61, 63, 73; and al-Ḥurr 6–7; martyrdom of 1–2, 20, 45–47; and Yazīd 22, 74; virtues of 24, 26–29, 31, 41, 48, 57–58, 62, 70, 79, 85

Ibn Khaldūn 52, 85
Ibn Ziyād, ʿUbaydallāh 7–8, 23, 31, 59–60, 62–63, 71, 74, 77
Iliad 2
Iqbal, Muhammad 29
Irbīlī, Abū al-Ḥasan ʿAlī 27
ʿirḍ see honor
Iron Man (2008) 42

Jaʿfar ibn Abī Tālib 28
Jesus 12, 30, 50–51, 56–57, 80
jihad 18, 69, 77–78
Judaism 12, 50–51

kāfir 36
Kant, Immanuel 13–24, 23–34, 44, 84
karam: defined 26–28; Arab 20, 30, 58, 60, 63; al-Ḥusayn as exemplar 27–28, 87; inherited 7; mindfulness of God 31; as virtue 29–30, 33; warrior nobility 3, 6, 34–35, 38, 47, 51, 55, 63, 69, 72, 74, 80, 85–86; Zaynab's 8, 32
Karbala, Battle of: as historical myth 11–22; and intimacy with God 45–47; lioness of 32; narrative 1–3, 7, 9, 12, 21, 23, 31–32, 38, 44, 70, 75–77, 80, 83; Paradigm 32–33; and sainthood 34–35; and virtue ethics 11, 14, 19–20, 26–29, 47–48, 58, 85–87; visitation 19; and warrior ethos 6, 8, 22, 41, 53, 55, 57, 60–61, 63; and Zaynab 77–79
Kāshānī, Muḥsin Fayḍ al- 28
Kāshifī, Kamāl al-Dīn Ḥusayn Wāʿiẓ 60–61
Keanu (2016) 3

Late Capitalism 43–44
Lawrence, Bruce B. 68
love: and ʿAlī 37–38; for God 28, 30, 85; God's 7, 19, 31, 36; and al-Ḥusayn 29; and Karbala narrative 58, 75; for Prophet's family 2

MacIntyre, Alasdair 2, 12–13
Mahallati, Mohammad Jafar Amir 22
Maldon, Battle of 55, 57–58, 80
manliness 4–5, 26, 47–48, 58, 61, 85; *see also* youngmanliness
maqtal 11
Markwith, Zachary 40n57
mātam 33
Matthews, Washington 84
Mill, John Stuart 13
Mitchell, Jeff 9, 24
Moses 12, 30–31, 45–47, 51, 87
Muhammad (Prophet): companions of 4; family 7–8, 27; and al-Ḥusayn 21, 28, 79, 87; Nietzsche's views of 49, 52, 69; nobility of 30; warrior ethos 17–19, 35, 58
Muḥāribī, ʿAlī ibn al-Ṭaʿʿān al- 70
Muḥarram 1–2, 32–33
Mukhtār ibn Abī ʿUbayd, al- 60
Muntaẓirī, Ḥusayn-ʿAlī 22
murūʿa 26, 47–48, 85; *see also* manliness
Muslim ibn ʿAqīl 23, 74

Nāṣir, al- (Caliph) 5
Navajo 84
Neoplatonism 30
Nietzsche, Friedrich 3, 5, 41, 47–58, 60, 63, 77, 84
nobility see *karam*
Nussbaum, Martha 14–17

Orientalism 49, 51, 86

Paul 50
Pharaoh 45–46
phronesis 14
Pink Floyd 43
pudicitia 5

Qaṣrī, Khālid ibn ʿAbdallāh al- 4

Rahimi, Babak 33
Ricoeur, Paul 53, 63
riḍā 28, 32
Ruffle, Karen 33–34
Rūmī (Jalāl al-Dīn Balkhī) 37

Schiller, Friedrich 54
Schopenhauer, Arthur 49–50
self-sacrifice 2, 8, 17–18, 20, 26–27, 41, 58, 71, 79, 87
self-worth 17, 20–21, 87
Semitic 49–51
Shāfiʿī, Kamāl al-Dīn ibn Ṭalḥa al-, 26–28
Shah-Kazemi, Reza 69
shahīd 67, 78
Shiʿi Muslims 2, 9, 11, 19, 35, 48, 67
Shuster,Joe 41
shuṭṭār 4
Siegel, Jerry 41
Singer, P.W. 72
Smith, Linda Tuhiwai 84
Sondy, Amanullah De 33
Sparrow, Robert 72–74
Spinoza, Baruch 51
Star Wars 42
Stoicism 29
Sufism 5, 29, 34, 36–37
Sulamī, Abū ʿAbd al-Raḥmān al- 36
Sunni Muslims 2, 26, 29, 37, 67
Superman 41
Szanto, Edith 33

Ṭabarī, al- 59, 70
taʿziyya 32
Tertullian 51
Thor 42
Thucydides 16
Ṭirimmāḥ ibn ʿAdī, al- 59
Top Gun: Maverick (2022) 42

ʿUbaydallāh ibn Ziyād 7–8, 23, 31, 59–60, 62–63, 71, 74, 77
Übermensch 41
ʿUmar (Caliph) 18
Umayyads 8, 18, 57, 60
Utilitarianism 13–14

Van Norden, Bryan W. 84
virtue ethics 11–16, 29, 34, 72, 86
visitation prayers and treatises see *ziyārāt, al-*

walāya/wilāya 34
Williams, Bernard 15, 76

Yazīd I (Caliph) 1–2, 8, 21–22, 28, 74, 77
youngmanliness see *futuwwa*

Zākānī, ʿUbayd 3
Zayn al-ʿĀbidīn 78
Zaynab bint ʿAlī 7–8, 31–34, 77–80, 85
Zeus 48
ziyārāt, al- 19, 34–35
Ziyārat al-Arbaʿīn 19
Ziyārat ʿĀshūrāʾ 19
Zuhayr ibn al-Qayn 6–7, 21